# THE BURNING OF EVELYN FOSTER

2

# THE BURNING
# OF EVELYN FOSTER

Jonathan Goodman

CHARLES SCRIBNER'S SONS
*New York*

Copyright © Jonathan Goodman 1977

Copyright under the Berne Convention

All rights reserved. No part of this book
may be reproduced in any form without the
permission of Charles Scribner's Sons.

1 3 5 7 9 11 13 15 17 19 I/C 20 18 16 14 12 10 8 6 4 2

Printed in Great Britain

Library of Congress Catalog Card Number 77-77803
ISBN   0-684-15306-8

*Dedicated*
*to the memory of*
*Robert F. Hussey,*
*for whom January 1931*
*had special significance,*
*and once again to Susan*

# PREFACE

It is an odd coincidence that the Wallace case, the classic factual 'who-dunnit', and the burning of Evelyn Foster, which is probably the most intriguing 'whatwasit', both happened in January 1931. Whereas several books have been devoted to the Liverpool murder case, among them my own *The Killing of Julia Wallace*, the Foster case has been discussed, or merely described, only in essays and articles. I feel fortunate in being the first author to examine the case at length—and, as I hope the reader will agree, in depth.

I should like to make it clear that my criticisms of the Northumberland Constabulary at the time of the Foster case do not apply to the present-day Northumbria Police Force, which is as efficient as any in the country.

All conversations in this book are either taken from records or based on the recollections of the principals questioned by myself.

The quotations heading chapters 2–6 are from the 'Sherlock Holmes' stories of Sir Arthur Conan Doyle (2, 'A Scandal in Bohemia'; 3, *A Study in Scarlet*; 4, *The Hound of the Baskervilles*; 5, 'The Sign of Four'; 6, 'The Dancing Men').

I am indebted to a great many people, but particularly to the Reverend Peter Brierley and his wife Kate. While I was researching and writing this book, Peter Brierley was Priest in Charge of Kirkwhelpington; he is now Vicar of Greenhead, near Carlisle.

I also wish to thank, among others:

Kenneth G. Oxford, Deputy Chief Constable of the Merseyside Police (previously Assistant Chief Constable [Crime], Northumberland Constabulary), and A. J. T. Anderson, of CID (Admin), Northumbria Police.

Henry Adams; B. Arthur, Northumberland County Surveyor; Trevor Atkinson, of the *Newcastle Daily Journal*; Charles Beattie; Roger Bolam, Assistant Editor of the *Newcastle Evening Chronicle*; James V. Borwick; Nick Bryden; Mrs M. Coulson; Mrs V. Elliott; Lorimer Farrell; Mrs Amy Ford (nee Johnstone); D. Foreman, Senior Librarian, Newcastle Chronicle and Journal Ltd; Miss Margaret Foster; Edward Groves and his wife Dorothy (nee Blackham); Edmund Hand; A. Henderson; Robert Henderson and his wife Lena (nee Middlemass); J. Henshaw, Chief Fire Officer, County of Northumberland; Cecil Johnstone; G. E. Laughton, Northumberland County Librarian; John Lilley, of the Photo Centre, Alnwick; Mrs E. Moore; Mrs Mary Nevin (nee Glass); Mrs Eileen Newcastle-Cleveland; Robert Pringle; Miss Jane Rowntree; Thomas Rutherford; Miss C. T. Sanders; Mr and Mrs Alfred Scott; Mrs E. Scott; E. Scott; Mrs Margaret Scott; J. V. Waddell, Director of Otterburn Mill Ltd; Mrs Judie Wick; Mrs Dorothy Wright (nee Foster).

Dr F. E. D. Griffiths; Dr P. T. d'Orban, Medical Officer of Parkhurst Prison; Dr Ian Pickering, Director of Prison Medical Services, Home Office; Dr Gavin Thurston; Dr D. O. Topp, of the Prison Department, Home Office; Dr C. L. Oakley, Archivist of the Royal College of Pathologists.

E. A. Bellamy, Librarian of the National Motor Museum at Beaulieu; A. P. Bird, Competition Secretary, the Vintage Sports-Car Club; W. Boddy, Editor of *Motor Sport*; Mrs Ellen S. Broad, Editor of *The Veteran and Vintage Magazine*; G. F. Collie; John S. Conde, Assistant Director of Public Relations, American Motors Corporation; W. G. Earley; R. N. Eason Gibson, Technical and Promotions Manager, the Royal Automobile Club; N. D. Hodgson; Bruce Jupp, of the Petroleum Industry Training Board; Donald Godwin Morris; Harry C. G. Shell, Hon. Secretary of the Classic American Auto Club of Great Britain; Roy Siddall; Ian Webb, Editor of *Milestones*; R. H. Weist, Editor of *Motor Trade Executive*; Jonathan Wood, of the editorial staff of *Classic Car*.

W. Adams, Establishment Officer for the Director of Public Prosecutions; Miss P. A. Fitzgerald, of the Home Office; Miss M. I. Hargreaves, of the Meteorological Office; J. Hutton, of the University of Durham; John L. Jablonsky, Assistant Vice President, Engineering & Safety Service, American Insurance Association; H. G. Pearson, Departmental

8

Records Officer, Home Office; Canon L. Lloyd Rees, Chaplain General of Prisons; G. B. Spence, of the Central Statistical Office.

Terry Boxall; George Burnett; Ivan Butler; Peter Cotes; Rayner Heppenstall; Mrs Pamela Jackson (nee Mitford); C. P. Kallender, Deputy Librarian of the *Daily Express*; Hector Munro; Lord Redesdale; Robert Rickard, Editor of *The News: a Miscellany of Fortean Curiosities*; Richard Whittington-Egan.

Lastly, I want to thank two editors: J. H. H. Gaute, who has taught me a great deal, and James MacGibbon, who is still teaching me.

JONATHAN GOODMAN
London, 1976

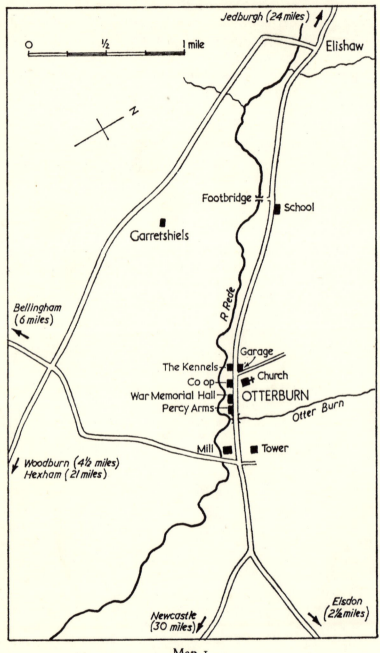

Map 1

# I

OTTERBURN, *village and parish, central Northumberland, on Red River and 18 miles north of Hexham; woollen milling. Scene of battle (1388) in which the Scots defeated the English; sometimes called the battle of Chevy Chase, after the ballad. A lonely gibbet can be seen 5 miles south-east at Steng Cross.*

The village has hardly changed at all since the early months of 1931, when photographs of the place were printed on the front pages of newspapers, seemingly inapt illustrations to reports concerning the cruel and mysterious death of a young woman—cruel because Evelyn Foster's death was caused by burning, mysterious because no one could be really sure whether this was a case of accident, suicide, or murder.

In describing Otterburn—as it was then, as it is now—the words 'was' and 'is' are usually interchangeable. There are some new buildings, most of all on the rising land behind the parish church; and one or two of the old grey-stone houses, built square and squat to withstand the harsh winds from the moors, have been vested with the so-called decoration of pebble-dash. But the changes are almost invariably additions: virtually nothing has gone of what Evelyn Foster knew at the end of her twenty-nine years of life in the village where she was born.

To understand something of what happened on the night of Tuesday, 6 January 1931, one needs to fix a picture of Otterburn, the relation of one building to another, in the mind. This doesn't require much concentration, for the village is small, barely more than a quarter of a mile from end to end; it is also compact, with none of the houses venturing far from the road which it straddles, and few venturing far along it. This road comes from Newcastle-upon-Tyne, 32 miles to the south-east, and goes on to Jedburgh, 26 miles away across the Scottish border; though the road continues north from Jedburgh, its route beyond the town need not concern us as it is of no apparent consequence to the Foster case.

If one enters the village from the direction of Newcastle, on the left-hand side of the road, and standing away from it in a lane, is Otterburn Mill, where fine tweed is woven from the wool of the black-faced sheep which graze on the local moors.

Across the road from the mill, but hidden by a high wall and trees, is a large battlemented house called Otterburn Tower; the foundations are said to be eleventh-century, but much of the present fabric dates from the early 1900s. It is now a hotel, but in 1931 the house was owned by Mrs Howard Pease, widow of the Northumberland historian; after her husband's death in 1928 (his grave is marked by a Celtic cross in a corner of the village churchyard), she used the house only infrequently, spending most of her time in London. She retained a small permanent staff, however, and among these was George MacDougall, who tended the grounds; his fingers were said to be so green that 'he could have grown prize geraniums in Abyssinia'. MacDougall's name will crop up again in this story.

Just beyond the Tower, an unobtrusive bridge takes the road over the Otter Burn, which, given impetus by a waterfall a hundred yards or so upstream, runs to the River Rede, meeting it on the far side of the mill. Across the bridge, on the left-hand side and set back from the road, is the Percy Arms. In 1931 the inn was only the first couple of houses in a block of half-a-dozen, but it has grown with the growth of tourism and now comprises the whole block. It is important to remember that, at the time of the Foster case, the entrance to the Percy Arms was no more than a few feet from the bridge; indeed, an arrangement to meet someone by the bridge would have been an arrangement to meet them in the cobbled forecourt of the inn. The closeness of the door of the original Percy Arms to the Otter Burn is indicated by the fact that a mark on the wall shows the height of the water on a Sunday night in 1907 when the burn overflowed and flooded the ground-floor rooms.

There is a wide yard next to the last of the houses in what I shall call 'the Percy Arms block'; in 1931 there was a blacksmith's shop at the foot of this yard—a favourite place for gossip, especially in the winter months—but the forge has long since disappeared.

On the other side of the yard, opposite a row of small white-washed houses and shops, is the War Memorial Hall, a long grey-stone structure with a corpulent porch jutting towards the road. Above the entrance are the names of nine men of Otterburn who lost their lives while serving in the 1914–18 war (only one name was added after World War II—that of Pilot Officer George Stephenson Waddell, the eldest son of the then managing director of the mill). For three days in February 1931 there can have been relatively few people in Britain, and perhaps none in Northumberland, who were unaware of the existence of the Otterburn Memorial Hall.

Next to the hall—and we are now halfway through Otterburn—is a cottage, more ornate than most of its neighbours, with lattice windows and a deeply sloping roof. Today a branch of Lloyd's Bank, it was for many years the post office, and in 1931 the sub-postmaster was Stanley Potts; his is another name that will recur.

And so will the names of George Sinclair and George Maughan, who at that time were manager and shop assistant respectively at the Otterburn District Co-operative Society's store, the next building along. The Co-op is a broad, flat-chested shop, the area in front of the counter being not much wider than the space behind. Tall windows on either side of a glass-panelled door, and utilitarian woodwork, make it look as much like a glass-house as a grocery shop. Thankfully, for drabness is infinitely more pleasing than neon or strip lighting, the directors have not thought it necessary to have the exterior vamped by shopfitters, who seem to think only in terms of voltage, never of appropriateness to the surroundings.

Across the road from the Co-op is the Anglican church of St John the Evangelist; early Victorian but discreet. The churchyard is raised a few feet from the level of the road, and steps lead up to it just beyond the lichgate, a diminutive structure that appears to have been designed to shelter only the coffins of midgets. The cluster of new council houses and bungalows behind the church is called Brierley Gardens in memory of the Reverend Joseph Philip Basil Brierley, the village priest from 1919 to 1949. The vicar had a family association with a celebrated murder case, for an uncle of his was the Alfred Brierley who perhaps unwittingly provided Mrs Florence Maybrick with the licentious one of her several motives for poisoning her husband in Liverpool in 1889.

Beyond the church and the Co-op, on both sides of the road, are a few more buildings before a sign shows the end of the 30mph speed limit through the village. Only two of these buildings, the last on each side, have a connection with the Foster case.

On the right, next to a subsidiary road that runs past Brierley Gardens, is a long stone-walled shed. Sign-written above the entrance facing the main road are the words:

THE

GARAGE

OTTERBURN

and below them the name of the owner, a Mr R. L. Corbett. The fairground colours of the sign are bright and unflaked by the wind, for until recently the garage was the property of the Foster family, whose home, The Kennels, is opposite, the first of two semi-detached houses with porches like swollen sentry-boxes, identified by a disused petrol pump set into the rough-stone wall that separates the garden from the pavement.

The road continues into open country on its way to Jedburgh, with occasional glimpses of the River Rede, twisting and turning but always running roughly parallel with the road, as it has done since it was entered by the Otter Burn.

A little over half a mile from the village, on the right, a path leads across a field to the Percy Cross (which is not a cross at all but a dart-shaped stone), marking the location, or near enough, of the battle between Scottish forces led by James, second Earl of Douglas, and an English army under the command of Hotspur—Sir Henry Percy—in the reign of Richard II. In the next field, beyond a small plantation of firs, is Otterburn School, which is situated here, a longish walk from the homes of its pupils, because some time in the middle of the nine-teenth century a man living in a house on the site started giving lessons to a number of village children; with the coming of compulsory elementary education in 1880, the house automatically became the school, and was eventually replaced by a more suitable building.

The headmaster in 1931 was William Blackham, and there was one other teacher, Miss Mary Ferry. Blackham's wife was the sister of George Sinclair, the manager of the Co-op. A second connection between the school and the shop was the fact that George Maughan, the assistant at the Co-op, had an evening job of cleaning the classrooms and, during the cold months, stoking the boiler for the radiators.

A mile farther on from the school is a spot known round about as Elishaw Road Ends (the local pronunciation makes Elishaw a rough rhyme for 'militia'), where the Otterburn-Jedburgh road is joined, on the left, by Dere Street, the Roman road from the south; it is possible, though hardly sensible unless one has time to spare, to return to Otterburn by way of Dere Street, because, about three miles from Elishaw, a road branches to the left and runs through to Otterburn Mill.

Elishaw is a bleak and desolate place, to all intents and purposes unremarkable except for the convergence of the two roads. But it has a special significance to the Evelyn Foster case, for if the story she told was true, then it was here, at Elishaw, that she first met the man who burnt her to death.

*It is a capital mistake to theorise before one has data.*
*Insensibly one begins to twist facts to suit theories,*
*instead of theories to suit facts.*

In 1931 there were two important trading families in Otterburn, one at each end of the village: the Waddells, owners of the mill, and the Fosters, who ran the garage. But trade was the only factor common to both families. Whereas the Waddells, by virtue of being old-established[1] and of engaging in a craft akin to art, had entered the social limbo of people known as the gentry, the Fosters were considered, and considered themselves, 'village people'.

This was due, at least in part, to the fact that a number of the villagers remembered Joseph Foster starting his business. He could pride himself on being a self-made man—but far more unusual, he had been a self-made *boy*, for it was in 1884, when he was only eleven, that he had first begun selling and repairing bicycles. More of the villagers remembered how Joseph, after training at the Daimler factory in the Midlands, had turned to motor vehicles in the early years of the century; it may be, though, that the success of the Otterburn Motor Car & Cycle Co had made these same villagers forgetful of how they had poked fun at the first of Joseph's new-fangled machines and prophesied his bankruptcy. In 1933, he wrote:

> At that time, people believed I was mad. Most of them thought they would get blown to bits if they travelled in a car. Farmers used to laugh at us when we paid £23 for one tyre; they said we could get a horse for as much. Pedestrians would pass us going up hills, then turn round and jeer. Often the cars used to run back on hills, and to prevent this, we had to put a drag on the wheel. Sometimes, when a car went into a ditch, it had to be taken to pieces to be got back home again. I once had a steam car that would go twenty yards and then stop for twenty minutes.

In 1904 Joseph took the first step towards realising his ambition of, as he put it, 'bringing the country to the town, and the town to the country,' by concocting a miniature open-topped bus from an old Daimler car and running a regular service for farmers to Newcastle market, leaving Otterburn each Monday morning at four o'clock to arrive in the city by six. This contraption, which was given the first charabanc licence in the county, was christened the 'blacking box' by the passengers on account of their grubbiness when they alighted, aching and stiff-legged, after the 32-mile journey. Joseph afterwards admitted that 'it did look rather like a box perched on its enormous wheels, each four feet in diameter; there was no windscreen to protect the passengers, who sat in two rows, five abreast, facing each other, but at the back we sometimes fixed up a great fan to keep off some of the dust'.

Despite its discomfort, the blacking box was rarely short of passengers, either on the 'farmers' run' to Newcastle or on any of the other services that Joseph soon introduced, and in 1908 he built another. The two Daimlers remained in service, on short runs, for some years after he bought his first conventional buses, the original blacking box clocking up 200,000 miles before it was sold, not for scrap but to be reinstated as a car, at the start of World War I.

By the late 1920s, with little competition from other bus companies and virtually none from the London North Eastern Railway (the nearest station was at Woodburn, a good five miles from Otterburn, south along Dere Street), the firm owned ten single-deck buses, most of them Albions, with which they operated three services plying to and from Newcastle by different routes, morning to night, at a return fare of 4s 6d; in addition, each Tuesday morning a bus set off from outside the War Memorial Hall for Hexham, where it was market day, and returned in the late afternoon.

The bus service was one source of profit to the Fosters. There was also the motor-repair side of the business, which, as Joseph was expert and inventive enough to fashion a part if none was available, could cope quickly with just about every type of vehicle from private car to farm tractor; and there was the sale of petrol from the pumps at the garage and outside The Kennels. Another of Joseph's successful ventures was the purchase of heavy wagons to transport agricultural machinery and to move artillery from the sidings at the Woodburn and Knowesgate railway stations to the Redesdale army camp at Rochester, north of Otterburn.

Especially in the early years, the success of the business was due almost as much to the determination and organising ability of Joseph's wife Margaret, a girl from Seaton Delavel whom he had married in 1899, as to his own flair and mechanical aptitude. On top of looking after the home and bringing up four children, she it was who dealt with the paperwork, who reminded him to make out work-sheets for jobs from customers who could afford to pay for them, and forced him to do so for work accepted from people who he considered could not. She also chevied him when she thought he was wasting his time—perhaps when she saw him chatting to Howard Pease, from the Tower, whose boyish enthusiasm for cars was manifested in frequent visits to the garage, or when she thought he had spent too long in the dog-run at the back of the house, indulging his one hobby, the breeding of old-English collies.

Joseph, as his youngest daughter remembers, was 'a terrible man for dogs'. The house was called The Kennels before the Fosters moved there in 1901, part of it having been used as such by the original owner, and this name remained appropriate, with often as many as a dozen dogs under Joseph's care. People in Otterburn recall seeing him drunk just once each year, always on New Year's Day, when he returned from exhibiting his collies at an annual show in Newcastle.

Joseph Foster could count himself fortunate in his choice of wife; equally, he was lucky in having children who made up a close-knit and contented family, and who, even before they left the village school, were helping, in one way or another, with the business.

In 1931, Gordon, the first-born, was in his early thirties; he was married, and lived with his wife Mary, a local girl, in a house towards the centre of the village. He was, in effect if not by title, the foreman of the garage and, with his father now fifty-seven, was more and more assuming control of the firm. But it appears that, while he had inherited his mother's talent for organisation and planning, he had little of Joseph's concern for what is nowadays rather inflatedly called the dignity of the worker, and still less of his father's gift for getting the best from men by using an ostensibly easy-going approach. These deficiencies would have been intensified by the severe unemployment in the north-east between the wars: men were willing to take low wages for long hours of work, and in some cases to travel far from home to find a job. (So many of Joseph Foster's employees came from outside Otterburn that he had converted one of three small houses he owned opposite the

War Memorial Hall into a 'bothie', where they ate, slept, and occupied their spare time when they could not afford to visit the Percy Arms.)

Gordon is remembered as a hard task-master by men who worked for Foster's in the 1920s and 1930s—and in the context of those times, a hard task-master was very hard indeed. Those who came off worst were the members of the bus crews, for Gordon was in complete charge of the service. Allowing for the extravagance of memory, it seems that it was not unusual for drivers and conductors to work more than a month without a day off, and no payment was made for this excessive overtime. According to Gordon's way of thinking, the 'Hexham drive' on Tuesdays was a day off for the crew, since the bus arrived at the market town at about half-past nine in the morning and did not leave until after four, giving the men more than six hours of leisure in which to take a nap in the bus, have tea at a café, look round the market-stalls, or augment the crowd at a livestock auction—even, if they were complete hedonists, to do all these things; when the bus returned to Otterburn, its destination boards were changed and the petrol tank refilled, and the same crew took it out again, this time on one of the Newcastle routes. (The feeling of grievance on the part of the crews came to a head on Easter Sunday, 1933, when the men signed a petition saying that they would not work on the bank-holiday Monday, one of the busiest days of the year, without the assurance that they would get an apart-from-Hexham day off each week. Gordon threatened to sack any man who did not report for work the next day, but none wavered, and he gave in to the demand.)

One does not know what Joseph Foster thought of his son's idea of industrial relations. When a friend suggested, in so many words, that he should restrain Gordon's autocracy, he replied that 'the boy must be given his head'. Perhaps this was a sensible long-term viewpoint, for certainly Gordon mellowed as he gained experience of authority, but it meant that, for the present, a peacemaker was needed; someone to give the men the feeling that they were working with, and not just for, the Foster family.

This role fell, probably without her realising it, to Evelyn, the eldest of the Fosters' three daughters. The other girls, Dorothy—who was twenty-two in 1931, working as a conductress and occasionally helping with the petrol pumps—and Margaret, who at twenty had been a conductress for three years, were too young to influence either the affairs or the working atmosphere of the firm. But Evelyn, as will appear, was in the singular position of being part of the firm yet apart from it, and because of this, was able to cut short, or at least gloss over, the scenes between her brother and the men. According to one of the drivers: 'If she happened to be in the garage or round about when Gordon was letting fly, she would come over to him and tell him she wanted to ask him something important. You didn't need glasses to see that he was dying to tell her to go away, but Evie would just stand there, and rather than have a family argument in front of the men, he would glare but go with her. When he came back, most of the steam had gone out of him.' Another man who worked for Foster's in the 1920s remembers: 'The first time I was hauled over the coals by Gordon, he did it front of everyone. I was just a young lad, and I didn't know where to put myself—whether to cry, run home, or what. Then, when Gordon was well out of the way, Miss Foster came over to me. She just smiled and said: "Take no notice of him," and walked on. That was all, but it was nice of her. . . . She always seemed happy, and some of it rubbed off on us.'[2]

Certainly as far as material things were concerned, Evelyn Foster seemed to have good reason to be happy. Though only twenty-nine (she was born on 20 November 1901), she had her own hire-car, and possessed money or disposable assests to the value of some £1,400—a sizeable sum in 1931, equivalent to about £12,000 today.

In most parts of the country, women drivers of taxi-cabs or hire-cars were, and are, rare; but in the Middle Marches of Northumberland, for fifteen years or so during and after the first world war, they were fairly commonplace. At Elsdon, four miles east of Otterburn, off the Newcastle road, a Miss Brannen ran a hire-car from the village inn, the Bird in the Bush. Another local chauffeuse was Mary Glass, who drove a car belonging to her father, landlord of the Railway Inn at Bellingham, a small town about eight miles south-west of Otterburn. Now in her eighties, she recalls:

Before the war, my father owned horses and traps which he hired out; he also owned a car, an American Ford. A man was employed to drive this car, which was used to transport visitors to the hotel and to take commercial travellers and doctors to various parts of the countryside. In 1914, it was decided that I should be taught to drive so as to take over the man's duties when he went to war; the car would then be needed much more as the horses would also be taken for the war. The man taught me to drive, and I took over his work, driving as far as Edinburgh, Newcastle and Carlisle. One of my duties was to transport bank officials to their various sub-branches. One of these was in Otterburn. I had to make this trip twice a week and wait in the village for two hours until the business was completed. While waiting, I would often call at the Fosters' garage, and so became friendly with the family. I got to know Evelyn very well, though she was often out driving her own car.

Evelyn Foster's hire-car business was an offshoot from the family firm, and was still connected with it in the sense that orders were taken at the office. The car was kept at the garage, where it was also serviced and replenished with petrol, Evelyn keeping a reckoning of the number of gallons she had taken and making periodic payments; and, because it worked out far cheaper, the car's insurance was covered by Joseph Foster's 'floating' policies for the firm's vehicles.

More by observation than tuition, Evelyn had learnt to drive before she left school. Since the early days of the firm, her father had run a hire-car on an extempore basis, as much to help friends and to build goodwill as to make money; but with the war, virtually all his time, and that of his reduced staff, was taken up with the integral functions of the business. The war, however, greatly increased the demand for a hire-car—chiefly by bringing hundreds of men to the Redesdale army camp—and Joseph, never one to look a gift-horse in the mouth, brought his Standard car into full-time service. At first, usually he or Gordon somehow found time to do the driving, and then, when Evelyn was no more than fifteen, she occasionally drove the car on short trips with passengers who were known to the family. Before long, she was doing as much driving as her father and brother together, and was no longer restricted in terms of mileage or type of passenger. That she was considered both an expert driver and a pleasant travelling companion is shewn by the fact that, within a short time, she had her own 'regulars', people who specified that they wished to be driven by her.

The progression was completed when she was in her early twenties. She became 'run down' after a dental operation, and the family's GP, Dr Miller of Bellingham, advised her parents that she should spend even more time out of doors. Her father bought her a car of her own, a second-hand 'tin Lizzie' Ford, and turned all his hire-car trade over to her. She continued to work for the family firm in short spells—usually as a 'fill-in' conductress on evening buses—but most of her energy went into what was now her own small business.

Joseph Foster's action in setting her up on her own was certainly generous, but not excessively so, for the war had been over for two or three years, and the Redesdale army camp was no longer jam-packed with troops; also, many more of the farmers in the area now had cars or vans. But, gradually, Evelyn Foster built up the business until it was almost back to the level of the war years. She is described by people who knew her as a quiet and reserved sort of girl; others speak of her determination. These traits, allied with her love of cars—which, according to one of her friends, 'seemed to make her light up when she was talking about them'—appear to have been the ingredients of an efficient 'soft-sell'. She managed, in large measure, to break down the feeling among poorer people—of whom Northumberland had more than its fair share—that to travel in a hired car was a luxury reserved for weddings and funerals. One of the ways in which she did this was based on a service operated for several years by her father, and now by herself: people alighting from the bus at Otterburn, but living some distance away, could crowd into the car and be dropped off at, or somewhere near, their respective destinations; each passenger paid a fraction of the complete fare. Evelyn extended the share-a-car principle to include transport home from dances or whist drives at the War Memorial Hall, and trips to and from shows at the Theatre Royal or cinemas in Newcastle (the last bus to Otterburn left the city soon after nine), local but inaccessible meetings of the Women's Institute, and a diversity of other functions.

In social contrast to the share-a-car passengers were the friends and kin of the aristocratic families with estates in the area. When there was a house-party, and during the shooting and fishing seasons, many of the guests travelled by rail as far as Newcastle or Woodburn, and Evelyn drove them on from there.

She worked a seven-day week; indeed, Sunday was especially busy as she had contracts to drive ministers of various denominations on their circuits of meetings and services about the countryside. One of her regular ecclesiastical passengers was a Presbyterian minister who preached to a small but undoubtedly committed congregation in a draughty shed called The Ark, at Byrness, between Rochester and Jedburgh; a couple of the other ministers were Revivalists, and they had no church at all, not even a shed, but held open-air or camp meetings in fields. If while being driven by Evelyn Foster, any of the preachers attempted to make her see their particular idea of the light, there is nothing to indicate that they met with the slightest success. A casual Christian (in the phrase of one of her sisters, 'not particularly religious, being Church of England'), she rarely, if ever, attended a service at the village church; she often, however, came into contact with Vicar Brierley, who had known her since she was seventeen and to whom she sometimes turned for advice on secular matters.

Evelyn Foster was a kind and generous person; there is no doubt about that. She would always stop her car and offer a lift to anyone she knew, even if only by sight, on the roads outside Otterburn. And people still living in or near the village who were children in the 1920s (Mrs Lena Henderson of Rochester is one) remember her taking them for picnics on fine summer afternoons: '. . . lemonade and chocolate digestive biscuits, and playing games with Evie in the fields, and the special excitement at the thought of getting in the car again for the drive home, while all the time you were wishing the afternoon would never end; those picnics were the highlights of the years.'

After the illness in her early twenties, Evelyn had no serious health problems—or, at least, none of which anyone else was aware—until June 1930, when an untended cut on her right hand resulted in septicae-mia; she was in pain for some weeks from the swollen and discoloured hand, and unable to work. Rather belatedly, it seems, she was admitted to hospital, where her little finger was lanced to discharge the pus; though this cured the trouble, it left the finger stiff at the joints.

If appearance is anything to go by, she looked robust enough. She took after the rest of the family in being of slightly less than average height, but was big-boned and inclined towards plumpness, which she sought to hide by wearing dresses that fell from the shoulders rather than fitted the figure. People who knew her claim that photographs do not do justice to her face—and there may be something in this, for the camera certainly lied about the colour of her hair, which appears in photographs as brunette although it was in fact a dusty blonde. All one can say is that she was pretty, but not strikingly so; that she had regular features and a high forehead that was accentuated by a gap at the centre of her hairline—an inverted widow's peak, as it were; and that in some of the photographs—snapshots as well as studio portraits

—one detects a calm brightness that, with only slight exaggeration, might be called madonna-like.

From about the age of eighteen, she had a few casual friendships with young men of the village, but not until she was in her mid-twenties did she start 'going steady' with anyone. There is no sure indication of why she waited, or was kept waiting, for her first romance. It may be that the local bachelors she met, most of whom were farmhands or mill workers, were a trifle overawed by the fact that she had her own business and that her family was far wealthier than theirs; on the other hand, she may have been put off by their parochialism and comparative naivety. Then again, her shyness may have been interpreted by some as lack of interest. So far as one knows, Evelyn's parents did not try to influence her choice of male friends—and, in any case, her determination was such that family interference would probably have had little, if any, effect.

Her first real boyfriend was a Scotsman, slightly older than herself, called Ernest Primrose. A native of Leith, near Edinburgh, he had served as a driver in the army, joining towards the end of the war and staying on for a few years afterwards, and had at one time been stationed at the Redesdale camp. After demobilisation, he got a job with Foster's as a bus-driver, and lived at the firm's bothie.

Evelyn first came into contact with him at the garage, then met him at dances in the War Memorial Hall. But what chiefly brought them together, and sometimes secluded them from people they knew, were Evelyn's duties as a 'fill-in' conductress on evening buses. Occasionally, she took over from Primrose's usual conductor, and if they were on the last run from Newcastle, they would often have the bus to themselves after the stop at Belsay, eighteen miles from Otterburn, or at Kirkwhelpington, seven miles farther on, and Evelyn would then relax on the long seat across from the driving partition and they would chat.

They went out together for more than a year—to village dances and for drives and strolls in the country—and once or twice Ernest was invited to Sunday dinner at The Kennels. But when the gossips at the forge were already speculating as to when the engagement would be announced, Evelyn broke off the relationship—or rather, by inventing excuses for not going out, let it dwindle away. No one is quite sure why she did this, and it could be misleading to repeat village surmise at the time and since; people tend to assign their own reasons to the decisions of others.

Ernest Primrose was clearly unhappy; and he must have been embarrassed, as much by the altered bus-crew schedules which ensured that Evelyn never again worked with him as by their chance encounters at the garage or in the village. Torn between unhappiness and unemployment, he continued to work for Foster's for a few months, then left and returned to Scotland.

Soon afterwards, Evelyn started going out with George Phillipson, a young man employed by the firm as a joiner; his main job was to look after the woodwork of the buses. As his home was at Wark, a small village on the Tyne, about ten miles from Otterburn, he lived at the bothie. It seemed that he and Evelyn were well-suited; he was quiet and unassuming, but far less diffident than she, and was liked by her family —especially Joseph, who had noted his good and conscientious work.

By January 1931, much of the talk in the blacksmith's shop was once more focussed on Evelyn Foster: on when—no longer if—she would wed George Phillipson. No one, not even the gossips most spendthrift with words, most adept at transforming small incidents and remarks into clues about other people's lives, considered as a fertile subject the question of whether she was truly happy and untroubled. Evelyn Foster's happiness was apparent; an unshadowed thing. That was the knowledgeable view, at any rate.

Reference Notes: Chapter 2

1 The lease of the mill was purchased in the summer of 1821 by William Waddell, who had come over the border from the village of Bedrule, outside Jedburgh, where he and his brother had carried on a similar business for some years. The present showroom is a queer mixture of commercial and ancestral, with oil paintings of the successive heads of the firm above the shelves holding the bolts of tweed.
2 Gordon Foster's surviving sisters dispute the criticisms of him as an employer. They agree that he had a quick temper, but contend that 'he found his temper as quickly as he lost it', and that, in any case, the behaviour of some of the men 'would have tried the patience of a saint'.

# 3

*Where there is no imagination there is no horror.*

Shortly before half-past six on Tuesday evening, 6 January 1931, the village street was lit by the headlamps of the bus returning from Hexham. The driver was twenty-eight-year-old Cecil Johnstone, good-looking and loquacious, known to virtually all who travelled on Foster's buses by his first name, which is pronounced with a long *e* in these parts. Slowing down as he crossed the bridge, he pulled into the forecourt of the Percy Arms, the last stop before the garage, and most of the remaining passengers got out. They were followed by the conductor, Tommy Rutherford, a stocky lad still in his teens, one of whose non-conducting duties on the market-day run was to pick up meat and groceries ordered by villagers from a Hexham store and drop them off in the hall of the Percy Arms.

On this particular Tuesday (and the fact is relevant to the story), one of the parcels contained a pound of best pork sausages which Miss Mary Ferry, the schoolmistress, would collect in about three-quarters of an hour's time. Miss Ferry was particular about many things—not least, the quality of the food she bought, most of it to be eaten by her brother, whose work at the mill gave him an appetite that dwarfed her own—and as the sausages sold at the Otterburn Co-op were inferior to the exacting standard she set, she often ordered them from the shop in Hexham.

As soon as Rutherford was back on the bus, Cecil Johnstone drove on towards the garage. It was a fine, still night, but bitterly cold, and the street was practically deserted. Most of the villagers were indoors by now, sitting in front of their fires or eating high tea; some were reading the *Evening Chronicle*, copies of which were brought in on one of the Newcastle buses (the headlines were placid today, none more exciting than VISCOUNT TO WED and TYNE STEAMER FAST ON SANDBANK); a few of the villagers and their children were probably engaged in the small

26

Twelfth-Night chore of taking down the tinselled reminders of Christmas.

At the garage, the last of the passengers left the bus. Most of them hurried away, but a woman and two men remained, standing inside the entrance of the garage, which gave them at least an impression of shelter from the cold.

Gordon Foster hurried out of the building. He looked across at Johnstone, who was leaning against the Albion bus which he would shortly take on the Newcastle run. 'Three going on?' Gordon asked.

'All for Rochester,' Johnstone replied.

Gordon crossed the road to The Kennels and went into the living-room, to the left of the front door. Joseph Foster was sitting at the table by the window, pricing the day's work-sheets; he murmured, 'Yes,' and nodded towards the kitchen, at the back of the house, when Gordon asked if Evelyn was in.

Gordon walked into the kitchen and saw his sister primping her hair in front of a mirror. She was wearing a loose-fitting jersey, a skirt and overcoat made of brown tweed that she had bought at Otterburn Mill, and a brown woollen scarf.

'There are some passengers for Rochester,' Gordon told her.

'Yes, I'm getting ready to go with them,' she said, putting on her brown felt hat.

A moment or so later, Cecil Johnstone saw her walk to the garage and get into her car. Since the 'tin Lizzie' Ford, the present from her father, Evelyn had had a succession of cars, all American—a Buick, a Dodge, an Overland, an Essex—and all bought second-hand. Her present car was American, too—a black 1928-model Hudson Super-Six saloon which she had obtained the previous year from Rossleigh & Co, a firm of motor dealers in Newcastle; she had paid just over £200 for it.

With her passengers—the two men in the back of the Hudson, the woman, Mrs Esther Murray, sitting beside her—Evelyn turned to the right outside the garage and set off on the journey of five miles or so, passing first the school, then Elishaw Road Ends, before arriving at the village of Rochester. The two men got out here;[1] Mrs Murray lived a couple of miles farther along the Jedburgh road, in one of the cluster of cottages that comprised Cottonshopeburn Foot, and Evelyn said that, as it was such a cold night, she would take her as far as Birdhopecraig

Hall, where the entrance made a good place to reverse the car for the drive back.

Mrs Murray, a talkative person, determinedly stayed in the Hudson to finish what she was saying while Evelyn backed off the road at Birdhopecraig. She saw a car pass, travelling in the direction of Otterburn; but though she afterwards racked her brains, she was unable to say what make or colour of car it was, let alone whether it was driven by a woman and had other occupants.

'I've brought a man down from Elishaw. He wants to go to Ponteland to catch the bus.'

According to Mrs Margaret Foster, those were her daughter's first words when she returned to the house at five or ten minutes past seven. The first words to her, that is. Evelyn may have said something to her father, still working at the table, as she passed through the living-room to the kitchen; this is unlikely, though, for paperwork tended to evaporate Joseph's usual benignity, and his daughters interrupted him only when it was really necessary—even then, they often asked their mother to interrupt on their behalf.

Mrs Foster asked Evelyn how she had met the man. Hurriedly, Evelyn explained that, on the way back from Birdhopecraig, she had been hailed by some people in a car standing at Elishaw Road Ends. She had pulled into the roadside, and a man had come over to her. He had told her that he had missed the Edinburgh–Newcastle bus at Jedburgh, but the people in the car, with whom he had had tea in the town, had given him a lift as far as Elishaw, where they were turning into Dere Street to go to Hexham; they had said that he could get a bus at Otterburn, and he had been about to telephone from the AA box.

Evelyn said she had told the man that the Newcastle bus had already left Otterburn, but that she would take him into the village and see about driving him the 24 miles to Ponteland,[2] where he could pick up a bus to Newcastle.

'What is he like?' Mrs Foster asked.

'Very respectable and gentlemanly-like,' Evelyn replied. 'He looks a bit of a knut.'

'Where is he now?'

'He has gone down to the inn to see if he can get a lift,' Evelyn explained, and added that the man had promised to leave word at the

Percy Arms in the unlikely event of his obtaining a free ride to Ponte-land or Newcastle. She went on to say that she had told him that she thought the hire-car fare to Ponteland would be about two pounds, but that she would check this at the garage. (Her uncertainty on this point was understandable: she had taken passengers to Ponteland in the past, but mileage was just one of three factors in reckoning the price, the others being the time of year, there being different rates for the 'high' and 'low' seasons, and the time of day, as there was a surcharge on journeys outside normal working hours.)

Mrs Foster remarked that two pounds seemed rather high, and Evelyn said: 'Get Daddy to work it out while I'm filling the car.'

During her absence—no more than a couple of minutes—Mrs Foster gave her husband a brief and incomplete account of what Evelyn had told her. Joseph's only question was why the man had not remained at the garage; but the fare to Ponteland—expensive anyway, and exaggerated by Evelyn—seemed sufficient reason for the man's hoping to find some cheaper means of transport. Joseph quickly worked out the price, and when Evelyn returned, told her that it was £1 16s od.

Dorothy, Evelyn's younger sister, had entered the living-room while her parents were discussing the transaction, and she now suggested that Evelyn should take George Phillipson with her.

'Oh, yes,' Mrs Foster said, 'do take him. Call and get him as you go through the village.'

'All right, Mother,' Evelyn agreed. Taking a flashlight from the mantelpiece, she left the house.

The time was about quarter-past seven.

An hour later, the Fosters' youngest daughter, Margaret, came home after conducting a bus from Bellingham. As she took off the heavy outer clothing which her mother had insisted on her wearing, she asked where Evelyn was, and casually mentioned that she had just seen George Phillipson in the village.

The last bus to Otterburn, driven by Cecil Johnstone, left the Hay-market terminus in Newcastle soon after nine. There was no need for headlamps, for the moon, not quite full, had risen at 8.20, and shone from a clear, star-flecked sky. Tommy Rutherford, the young con-ductor, collected the fares of the few passengers, none of whom was travelling far along the route, then huddled against the driving partition, hoping to receive some warmth from the engine.

Eight miles to Ponteland; another five or so to the smaller village of Belsay; seven more to the turning on the right leading to Kirkwhelpington, the tower of its thirteenth-century church visible from the main road, where the rich green lowlands began to give way to the moors stretching to the border.

The bus was now empty of passengers. Cecil Johnstone had not seen a moving vehicle or a pedestrian since round about Belsay, and he remarked to Rutherford that he wouldn't be surprised if they had the road to themselves right through to the garage.

He applied the hand-brake and got up, nodding to Rutherford to take his place at the wheel. It was against regulations for a conductor to drive a bus, but many of the crews broke the rule at one time or another when they were without passengers; Rutherford hoped to be promoted to bus-driver before long, and he welcomed the chance to increase his driving experience, albeit illicitly.

Johnstone sat behind the driving partition and lit his pipe. But he did not relax completely: he watched for lights on the road ahead or reflected in the side mirror, and kept an eye on the speedometer and the dashboard clock to make sure that the bus stayed on schedule. They passed the stone quarry at Knowesgate, about a mile and a half from Kirkwhelpington, at five minutes to ten; exactly on time. The road was still deserted.

For some two and a half miles after Knowesgate, Rutherford had to press slightly harder on the accelerator to retain the same speed as the road rose—not steeply, never enough for a change of gear—to a place known locally (but not, it seems, to any cartographer) as Wolf's Nick —a hummock with a slice cut from the spine to let the road pass through. Here, so it is said, the last wolf in the district was killed—the same animal, perhaps, from which a jutting piece of rock, 400yd from the road, derives its name of Wolf's Crag.

Though near the edge of the moors, the area beyond Wolf's Nick was, and is, as barren and wild as any of the moorland closer to Scotland. The ground, undulating on both sides of the road, was thatched with bracken and heather, and scattered with boulders and small rocks; a few elms managed to survive, looking in winter like fingerprints on the sky. The northern horizon was formed by the ridge of small hills called the Ottercops, and on one of these hills, about two miles north of Wolf's Nick, was a shepherd's cottage, the only building in sight apart from one or two farm sheds.

As Rutherford drove the bus through Wolf's Nick, he was concentrating on the road's gradual left-turn, so it was Johnstone who first noticed an intense red and orange glow on the frost-encrusted moors to the right. Johnstone jumped up, shouting to Rutherford to stop and at the same time leaning across to pull on the hand-brake. The bus came to a halt, and Johnstone and Rutherford stared through the side windows at the weird light.

After a moment, Rutherford murmured that perhaps some campers were kindling a fire.

'A bloody big camp-fire,' Johnstone replied dismissively. He only wished that he could think of some more plausible explanation. Managing to sound braver than he felt, he said that they had to go out and investigate.

But Rutherford, already shaken by Johnstone's shout and the sudden stop, was too young to hide his fear. It was a superstitious fear: the red and orange glow conjured memories of stories he had heard from his father, and not so long ago—stories of witches' sabbats, of hobgoblins, of lights that lured travellers to the dominion of the devil. He wasn't leaving the bus, he said.

Cecil Johnstone hesitated a second, then opened the door and stepped down to the road. It was the coldest night in Northumberland for two years,[3] and the frosty air bit into his face, making his eyes water, as he ran round the front of the bus and slithered down the short, sloping embankment on to the moors. He ran no more than a few steps across the heather, then stopped as he discerned the outline of the object from which the glow was coming and recognised it as that of a burnt-out car. He later realised that the main reason why neither he nor Rutherford had been able to identify it from the bus was because the glow came from the inside, and some of the dark patches of heather in the background had merged with the charred outline, making it amorphous from a distance of thirty or forty yards. Their eyes may also have been confused by the slightly fore-shortening angle of the car, which was facing towards Otterburn but diagonally to the road.

Johnstone ran the rest of the way to the car. The only part of it still on fire was a rear wheel. The small darting flames illuminated the registration plate, and Johnstone was able to make out the number: TN 8135.

It was a number that he knew well. The car was Evelyn Foster's Hudson.

This shock was followed by another, as a hand gripped his shoulder. He lurched round, only to find that Tommy Rutherford had decided that being on the moors with a companion was preferable to staying on his own in the bus.

Johnstone needed a moment or so before he felt able to speak, then he pointed at the registration plate: 'It's the firm's new Hudson,' he exclaimed.

The near-side windows of the car had melted, but the two doors were shut, and the heat made it impossible to get close enough to see the whole of the inside. Johnstone went round to the driver's side, where he found both doors open. Dreading what he might see, he shielded his eyes and looked at the seats and the floor; but the car was empty.

With a sense of tremendous relief, almost elation, he started back to Rutherford. A sound, slight but distinct, stopped him in his tracks. Looking at Rutherford, he saw that he, too, had heard it—a keening moan from somewhere in front of the car.

Slowly, hesitantly, the two men walked in the direction of the sound, and almost at once saw a dark shape on the ground nine or ten yards from the car. As they approached, they heard another slight moan. They stopped and for a moment stood staring at a twisted figure, unable or unwilling to believe that they were looking at Evelyn Foster, unable or unwilling to comprehend the horror of what they saw.

She was lying on her right side but with her face to the ground, and there was a slow rhythmic movement of her head as she licked the ice; her left arm was outstretched, the hand gripping a clump of bracken. She was naked from the waist down—even her shoes were gone—and the front of her body, from below the seared and tattered ends of her jersey to the knees, was a mass of dreadful burns; in places at the edge of the area of burning, the material of her clothing had coalesced with the skin to form fungus-like lumps. The burns continued, but less severely, below the knees, and it seemed that only her left foot had escaped the flames.

Cecil Johnstone pulled off his overcoat. Kneeling beside the girl, he wrapped the coat round her waist and legs, then gently prised the fingers of her left hand from the bracken. He had had too many shocks during the past few minutes, and he felt no emotion as he saw that the fleshy part of the palm of the hand was almost completely burnt away. Tenderly, he raised her shoulders from the ground. As he did so, the smell of burnt flesh made his stomach lurch; he retched, but somehow managed not to vomit.

In the moonlight, Johnstone could not see whether her face was burnt; it was swollen, especially around the eyes, which were no more than slits, but he could not make out more than that. He stroked the hair from her brow, and found that it was harsh and friable; locks of it fell away at his touch.

She looked at him, but without recognition, and he said: 'It's me, Evie—Cecil Johnstone.'

Her lips moved slightly as if she were repeating his name.

'Is anyone else here?' he asked.

'Oh, that awful man,' she muttered.

'What man?'

'He has gone in a motor-car.'

Johnstone asked no more questions. 'It's all right now,' he told her. 'We're taking you home.'

'If you'll lift me up, I'll try and walk to the bus,' she said.

But Johnstone doubted whether she would be able to stand, let alone walk. He carefully picked her up in his arms and, with Rutherford running ahead to open the door, carried her to the bus. They sat her on the first of the near-side seats facing the front, and lifted her legs on to the seat running parallel with the door. Fearing that she might lose consciousness during the drive, Johnstone threaded his scarf under her arms and tied the ends to the steel rail on the back of the seat. All the time she was groaning and looking at her hands, and she kept asking for water; once or twice she repeated the first thing she had said on the moors: 'That awful man.'

Johnstone could see now that her face, as well as being suffused and swollen, had several bad burns, especially on the cheeks, but that, despite the fact that there were burn-holes all over what was left of her jersey, there was no trace of burning under her chin or on her neck. Her eyebrows and eyelashes were gone, and the skin around her eyes was marked and discoloured. It looked to Johnstone as if 'the flesh had been made black and blue with blows'. Rutherford, too, noticed the 'bad black marks' and felt sure that they were 'inflicted wounds'.

Johnstone drove the bus faster than it had ever been driven, faster than it would ever be driven again, on the six-mile journey to Otterburn. On the way, he stopped at a roadside cottage where long-distance transport drivers spent the night, and Rutherford got Evelyn some water, which she drank painfully but greedily.

As the bus entered the village, Johnstone automatically glanced at the dashboard clock. The time was half-past ten. He was fifteen minutes behind schedule.

Hearing the distinctive sound of the engine of the bus, Gordon Foster looked at his watch and remarked that Johnstone was late back from Newcastle.

He and his wife were sitting in the living-room of The Kennels with his parents and Dorothy; his other sister, Margaret, had just gone to bed. It had been a pleasant family evening. He had discussed a few business matters with his father, but the rest of the talk had been inconsequential. Evelyn's trip to Ponteland had been an early topic, and a couple of times in the past hour one or other of the family had wondered what was keeping her out so late. But none of them had felt concern; they had assumed that she had either picked up another passenger after taking the man to Ponteland or had returned to the village and met George Phillipson.

The sound of the bus pulling up was followed by that of running footsteps on the path to the house; then there was the slight scuffling sound of someone opening the front door, which was always kept on the latch until the last of the family went to bed.

The door of the living-room opened and the Fosters saw that their late-night visitor was Cecil Johnstone. His face was pale, and he looked exhausted. 'Gordon, come here,' he said, and at once turned and walked out of the house.

Gordon hurried after him. 'What's the matter?' he asked.

Johnstone nodded towards the bus. 'Evelyn's here, badly burnt.'

Dorothy had come out to see what was happening, and as her brother ran to the bus she followed him, pulling away from Johnstone as he tried to stop her. By the time she entered the bus, Gordon was

WOMAN MURDERED ON LONELY MOOR

A page from the *Illustrated Police News* of 15 January 1931. A successor to the nineteenth-century crime broadsheets, this weekly journal was not noted for accuracy in its pictorial reporting.

already sitting beside Evelyn; she vaguely noticed that Tommy Rutherford was untying a scarf from the back of the seat.

'What has happened?' Gordon asked Evelyn.

'It's that man,' she replied.

'What, the one you took to Ponteland?'

'Yes. He has burnt me and the car.'

Gordon asked her what the man was like.

'He is about your build,' she said, 'and he is a little taller and not
quite so stout.[4] He had a bowler hat on. He was dark, and wore a dark
coat.'

Joseph Foster was approaching the bus, Johnstone by his side, as
Dorothy ran back to the house, where her mother was standing at the
door with Gordon's wife. Dorothy quickly told her mother what she
had seen and heard. The impact of the tragedy would strike Mrs
Foster later, but for the time being her mind was taken up with what
needed to be done to help Evelyn. She told Dorothy to telephone for a
doctor, and sent her daughter-in-law to ask the next-door neighbour,
Mrs Christian Adeline Jennings, to come to the house; then she ran
upstairs to waken Margaret and to get the bed ready in Evelyn's room,
directly above the living-room.

Contacting a doctor was easier said than done. The Fosters' own
doctor was out on a call when Dorothy telephoned, and most of the
other medical men in the area were at a Twelfth-Night dance. She
eventually got through to Dr Duncan McEachran, who had recently
qualified and was assistant to a Dr Kerr at Bellingham; he said that he
would come as quickly as possible. Dorothy then telephoned the
district nurse at Elsdon, and said that she would send a car to collect her.

As Dorothy finished this call, her father walked unsteadily and
apparently aimlessly into the house. She asked him if he was all right,
and he nodded and murmured that Evelyn wanted something to drink,
so he was going to make her some coffee. He moved towards the
kitchen, then turned back to ask if anyone had telephoned the police.
Dorothy replied that she had not done so and did not think that anyone
else had. Joseph said that he would put the kettle on and then call the
village constable, whose house was at the far end of Otterburn.

By now, Gordon had gone into the garage to question Johnstone
and Rutherford, leaving Evelyn in the bus with Thomas Vasey, the
motor mechanic on the night shift. Vasey, a tall, strongly-built man,

was a late-comer on the scene. He had been working on a vehicle at the rear of the garage when Johnstone's bus returned, and had finished off what he was doing before walking to the bus to find out if it needed any servicing for the following day; as he had entered the bus, Gordon had brushed past him, saying only that he was to stay with Evelyn.

Kneeling beside her, Vasey stared at the burns. 'What has done this?' he asked.

'He threw something over me and set me on fire in the car,' she replied.

Vasey asked if there was anything he could do for her.

'Oh, Tommy lift me up, lift me up,' she said weakly.

The mechanic cradled her in his arms and carried her across to the house and up to her room.

Meanwhile, Dorothy had gone to the garage to ask Gordon to send a car for the nurse. Seeing Vasey carrying Evelyn from the bus, Gordon told Cecil Johnstone to drive the vehicle to Elsdon; then he followed Dorothy back to the house.

As Johnstone reversed the bus, he saw Tommy Rutherford standing alone by the entrance to the garage. The youngster was shivering—perhaps not only from the cold, Johnstone thought; he himself had had 'a fit of the shakes' earlier on, a natural enough reaction to the events of the past three-quarters of an hour. He shouted to Rutherford to get in the bus, and set off for Elsdon.

For a few minutes after the sound of the engine died away, the village was silent, the street deserted; people's shadows passed across the bright windows of The Kennels, but there was no other movement.

It was a cheerful, neat room. The walls were covered with a flowered paper, and there were cretonne curtains over the window that looked out across the road to the garage; the glass globe, painted with a daffodil design, gave an amber tint to the light from the oil-lamp suspended from the centre of the ceiling. A few small ornaments of glass and pottery glistened on the dressing-table by the window, and there was more bric-à-brac—souvenirs of summertime trips to Redcar, Newbiggin, Whitley Bay—on the mantelpiece above the fireplace in the wall to the right of the window. The door was in the opposite wall, and right of it, facing the fireplace, was Evelyn's bed.

There were four women already with Evelyn when Dorothy entered the room. Mrs Foster and her daughter-in-law had taken Evelyn from Vasey, who had now gone downstairs, and were trying to make her comfortable on the bed while Margaret and Mrs Jennings, the neighbour, looked on.

'What has happened?' Mrs Foster asked her.

'Oh, it has been that man,' Evelyn said. 'He hit me and burned me.'

Trying to remember some incident that might explain what had happened as an act of revenge, Dorothy could only think of Evelyn's jilting of Ernest Primrose. 'Was it Ernest who did this?' she asked.

'Of course not,' Evelyn whispered. 'I don't know who the man was.'[5]

Mrs Foster asked her why she had not taken George Phillipson with her, as she had promised before leaving the house, and she replied that she had not seen him when she drove through the village.

Then: 'I am cold, Mother,' she said, 'and something is hurting my back.'

Before covering her with the bedclothes, Mrs Foster took the overcoat from the lower part of her body. It seems that, though Johnstone had told both Joseph and Gordon of the dreadful burns on her stomach and thighs, the information had not been passed to anyone else; until now, the women in the room had assumed that the overcoat was simply a makeshift blanket. They were unprepared for the terrible sight that was revealed when it was taken away. Their anguish was so intense that, afterwards, none of them would be able to recall how she or any of the others reacted at that moment; their eyes focussed unwillingly on the burns, and the horror of the sight shut out all other thoughts.

The nightmare picture would remain vivid in the women's minds for the rest of their lives. More than forty years later, Dorothy would describe what she had seen—what she still saw—in these words:[6]

'The burns were cruel—so bad that you could scarcely believe that you were looking at part of a human being. The flesh looked like a burnt sausage, and in places the skin had burst, just like a sausage when it is overdone. Between the thighs, where the burns were worst of all, the skin had gone hard and calloused, like the crackling on pork.'

Cecil Johnstone returned with the district nurse soon after eleven o'clock, and she was taken up to the bedroom. Realising at once that the burns on Evelyn's body were beyond treatment and that only a strong drug could deaden their pain, she began to apply ointment to the facial burns. But Evelyn pleaded: 'Never mind my face—just dress my legs.' Though it was futile, the nurse did as she was told, and was still engaged in this pretence of treatment when Dr McEachran arrived.

The young doctor treated Evelyn for shock and helped the nurse to finish dressing the burns. At about quarter to twelve, he was joined by Dr Miller, the Fosters' own doctor, who had driven from Bellingham in response to a message that Dorothy had left with his wife. Miller, an elderly man who had known Evelyn since she was a child, had to turn away from the bed to hide his emotion when she whispered that she was sorry that he had been called out on such a cold night. After a few minutes, the doctors briefly conferred; then McEachran asked Mrs Foster and Dorothy, the only members of the family now in the room, to accompany him and Dr Miller downstairs, leaving Evelyn with the nurse and Mrs Jennings.

In the living-room, McEachran told the family that there was no hope of Evelyn's recovering. Mrs Foster turned to Dr Miller and asked if there was really nothing that could be done. He shook his head and said: 'It is amazing that she can talk. But I wish for her sake that she were not so strong. All we can do is hope and pray that she doesn't rally.' He added that the police should be told to come as quickly as possible, while Evelyn was still able to answer questions.

Though there had, in fact, been what is nowadays referred to as a 'police presence' in the vicinity of the house for about an hour, it is not surprising that Dr Miller was unaware of it, for the presence was so discreet as to be almost invisible to the naked eye.

At quarter to eleven, after receiving Joseph Foster's telephone call, Andrew Fergusson, the village constable, telephoned the police station at Bellingham and relayed what he had been told to Police Sergeant Robert Shanks, who said that he would come to Otterburn at once. Fergusson, who was a hefty, blunt-featured man of thirty-five, then left the police house, which was near the mill, and made his way to the far end of the village—but, instead of going to The Kennels, where Joseph was waiting for him, he went into the garage. One cannot say for sure how long he was there before being espied by Thomas Vasey; it seems that it may have been anything between five minutes and a quarter of an hour.

(Unfortunately, Fergusson, who retired from the Northumberland County Constabulary more than twenty years ago and now lives at Seaton Burn, near Newcastle,[7] cannot remember a single detail of what he or anyone else did that night. There may be a psychological explanation for his partial amnesia—something to do with the trauma of being expected to take the initial steps in a possible murder inquiry when the most serious offences he had previously had to deal with were poaching, sheep-stealing and after-hours drinking at the village inn. Deep emotional shock may also explain the impression he created that night among the Fosters and their employees of having decided that modesty was the better part of valour—that it was better to do nothing than to risk doing the wrong things, or the right things wrongly. Having put forward a possible excuse for Fergusson's apparent dilatoriness, it may as well be said now as later that the police investigation of the Foster case was characterised by *quite inexcusable* procrastination, sins of omission, and buck-passing.)

Summoned to the garage by Vasey, Joseph and Gordon told the constable the one or two things they themselves knew and the several things they had heard from others concerning the events of the night. Though the account was full of gaps and ambiguities, Fergusson asked few questions, and it seemed to Joseph that he was only half listening. When Gordon asked him if a search had been started for Evelyn's assailant, he did not reply. Gordon pressed him for an answer, pointing out that Evelyn's rough description of the man should be circulated to all police stations in the area, but Fergusson evaded the question by saying that he was sure that Sergeant Shanks had everything under control and that Gordon and his father could speak to him as soon as he arrived from Bellingham.

Lacking his own means of transport, Shanks drove to Otterburn in a hired car, reaching the village at half-past eleven. If Joseph and Gordon Foster thought that, with his arrival, there would be a sudden flurry of police activity, they were disappointed. After a brief, whispered conversation with Fergusson, he asked them to repeat the account they had given the constable; then, muttering to himself and making no attempt to look less than flummoxed, he wandered across to Johnstone's bus. Johnstone and Rutherford had been sitting in the bus all this time; as they saw Shanks approaching, they got up, thinking that they were about to be interviewed. But no: the sergeant simply stared at the bus

40

for a moment, seemingly oblivious of their presence, then turned to Fergusson and instructed him to telephone Police Superintendent Thomas Shell, the head of the Hexham division, of which Otterburn was part.

As Fergusson started off towards the police house, Joseph Foster, his patience exhausted, grabbed the constable's arm and shouted that there was a perfectly good telephone at The Kennels. Imperturbably, Fergusson pulled his arm away and, with a nod of approval from Shanks, continued his walk to the other end of the village.

In the quarter of an hour while Fergusson was away, Joseph and Gordon returned to the house, and Shanks seems to have done nothing except wander around outside the garage, trying to make up his mind about what ought to be done. He was still waiting for inspiration when Fergusson returned, just before midnight.

It was now that the investigation at last got under way. Dr McEachran came across from the house to tell the two policeman that if they wanted to interview Evelyn Foster, they must do it at once. No doubt the idea of questioning the victim struck them as rather novel, but they agreed that it probably had merit. In any case, if they were wrong, they could always say that it was the doctor's idea, not theirs.

Six people were at Evelyn Foster's bedside when she was questioned: her mother, the two policemen, both doctors, and the district nurse.

Shanks ordered Fergusson to sit near the head of the bed and conduct the interview. After asking only a couple of questions, however, Fergusson complained that he found it difficult to hear Evelyn's answers, so Shanks said: 'Let Mrs Foster ask the questions.' Thus it was that, apart from some prompting by either Shanks or Fergusson, the responsibility for virtually the entire 'police interview' was handed over to the victim's mother.

It is hard to make any sense of this. The idea of changing the questioner as a means of increasing the audibility of the person being questioned is not one that would occur to most people in a month of Sundays; the almost automatic reaction would be to ask the person being questioned to try to speak up. Fergusson was never asked why he did not do this—but a possible reason why Shanks did not suggest that he should is that Evelyn Foster's answers to Fergusson's questions were perfectly audible to everyone in the room apart from the constable;

Shanks could hardly suggest that a dying girl should be asked to shout for the benefit of one person among six. Dr McEachran, in his evidence at the inquest, stated that, despite Evelyn's terrible injuries and the suffering she endured, her speech was 'not at all affected' and that she was 'quite lucid and sensible in her understanding'. From the time she was found at Wolf's Nick until her death, she spoke to, or in the presence of, about a dozen people—and, of these, only Fergusson experienced difficulty in hearing what she said. Oddly enough, Fergusson's impediment of hearing was cured as soon as he was relieved of the task of interviewing Evelyn, and one cannot help wondering whether his professed inability to hear her answers masked an inability at that moment to think of any questions.

The interview, if one can call it that, lasted twenty minutes or so. Mrs Foster explained at the inquest: 'When I asked a question, Evelyn kept on answering. Her statements were partly answers to questions and partly voluntary.' Unfortunately, there is no way of knowing which questions were suggested by the police—nor, indeed, whether the prompting came from Shanks or Fergusson (at the inquest, Mrs Foster was not asked to identify the prompter; Dr McEachran said that it was Fergusson; Fergusson said that it was Shanks; and Shanks, whose presence for once would have been invaluable, was not called as a witness).

In the following account, Evelyn Foster's statements are pieced together into a roughly chronological order of the events she described; it should be remembered, however, that the sequence of the interview must have been far less tidy, and that one is almost wholly reliant on Mrs Foster's memory for points of detail, since the police made little attempt to record these.

It seems that none of Evelyn's statements concerning how she met the man at Elishaw and drove him into the village conflicted with the hurried explanation she had given her mother when she came into the house soon after seven o'clock to ask about the fare to Ponteland (see page 28).

She said that she had not noticed the registration number of the car from which the man alighted at Elishaw; all she could say was that the car was dark-coloured and closed.

Her statement about the occupants of the car was ambiguous. Mrs Foster told the coroner: 'She said there was a woman in the driver's seat of the car, and two men were in the car—but whether she meant two men besides the one who got into her car, I don't know.' Fergusson's note of the interview shows that his understanding was that only two people—the woman driver and a male passenger—remained in the car: 'There was a lady in the car with *a man* in it. The man [who had alighted] had had something to eat with *these people* at Jedburgh.'

Evelyn was asked few questions concerning her conversation with the man during the drive from Elishaw to Otterburn—and none at all, it seems, to explain whether, after leaving The Kennels and driving to the Percy Arms, she saw the man waiting for her, parked until he appeared, or went into the inn to find him (however, Dr McEachran stated at the inquest that Evelyn spoke of 'picking the man up on the bridge', which suggests that he was waiting there when she arrived).

She said that, with the man sitting next to her, she drove towards Ponteland. He smoked a lot of cigarettes during the journey. Their conversation was chiefly about cars, and the man mentioned that he owned one. Though he spoke with an accent that was 'like Tyneside—not broad Tyneside but north-country', he told her that he lived in the Midlands and did not know much about Newcastle.

After travelling 18 miles, they reached the village of Belsay. It was here, Evelyn said, that she first had reason to feel suspicious of the man. At the inquest, Mrs Foster recalled:

'She said she went through Belsay. I then said: "Are you sure?" She replied: "Yes, Mother, because I met two cars coming from Newcastle which I thought I knew. One was Mr Kirsopp-Reid's *[William Kirsopp-Reid owned a farm near Otterburn Mill]*; the other I was not sure of." She told me that when she reached Belsay, she said to the man: "Well, there is no bus here, but there will be one farther on." The man replied: "We will turn here and go back." Evelyn said she asked the man: "Why go back when you have come so far?" and he replied: "That's got nothing to do with you." *[Fergusson noted this reply as: "You have nothing to do with it."]* She said she turned the car, and afterwards felt the man creep along the seat towards her. He took hold of the steering-wheel and said he would drive back. She replied: "Oh, no; I will do the driving." He then took his hand and hit her over the eye. "Coming through Belsay," she said, "I looked out of the car to see if anyone was about in the village, but I couldn't see very well because my eye felt as if it was full of sand." I asked her if she did not

43

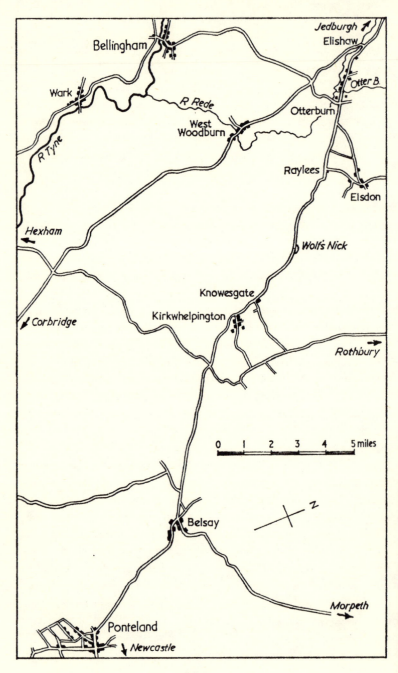

Map 2

try to stop and phone. To this she raised her voice and said: "I couldn't, Mother; I couldn't"—as though I didn't understand her position.'

Mrs Foster thought her daughter meant by this last remark that the man was sitting close up to her, pinioning her against the door, as he drove back along the road.

Evelyn said that the man stopped the car at Wolf's Nick, twelve miles from Belsay, and offered her a cigarette. She refused it, and he said: 'You are an independent young woman.' If Mrs Foster's recollection of the interview was correct, Evelyn stated that the man, after making this apparently casual remark, suddenly attacked her again:

'Evelyn told me: "Then he began hitting me, knocking me about. He knocked me into the back of the car." *[According to Fergusson's note. Evelyn's words were: "He struck me twice and knocked me into the back of the car. He did not appear to be drunk, but smelt a bit."]* She said the man kept nipping her arms. I asked her what happened in the back of the car—had he interfered with her? She replied: "Yes, Mother." I then exclaimed: "Oh, my God!" My daughter said: "Oh, Mother, I couldn't help it. I fought for my life."

'She said: "After that, he took something out of his pocket and threw it over me. I don't know whether it was out of a bottle or out of a tin. Then it went up in a blaze." She didn't know how it was lighted. She remembered nothing more until she felt a bump, which seemed as if it was caused by driving over rough ground; it roused her, and she got out of the car, but how she got out she could not remember. Then she heard a motor-car, but no one came across. The car went away. She didn't know which way it went. *[Fergusson recorded Evelyn's words as: "I heard a car pull up and someone whistle while the car was on fire." Dr McEachran remembered Evelyn saying that she also heard an explosion while she was lying on the ground.]* "How long were you there?" I asked her. She replied: "I couldn't say, Mother; it was a long, long time. I was so thirsty, I lay and sucked the grass." '

The interview ended at about half-past twelve, and Shanks and Fergusson left the house. It seems apparent that, before leaving, they did not discuss what they had heard; if they had done so, they could hardly have failed to realise that further questions needed to be asked, the answers to which could have closed some gaps and perhaps reconciled some of the inconsistencies in Evelyn's account—or in their understanding of it. They had been told that Evelyn was dying; they knew that this was almost certainly the last opportunity to question her; they must have understood the vital importance of getting as clear an account as possible—yet they ended the interview (or, more likely, allowed Mrs Foster to end it) without considering whether the questioning was complete.

Another policeman, Constable Henry Proud, had arrived on a bicycle from Bellingham soon after midnight, and he joined Shanks and Fergusson when they came out of the house. Their conversation was interrupted by Gordon Foster, who came across from the garage to tell them that he had instructed Thomas Vasey and Cecil Johnstone to drive to Wolfe's Nick to examine the burnt-out Hudson; he suggested—apparently without sarcasm—that if the police were thinking of visiting the scene of the crime that night, they might like to go with Vasey and Johnstone. Gordon's offer was accepted, if not enthusiastically, at least unanimously: though it would have been more sensible if two of the policemen had gone, leaving the third at The Kennels, all three crammed into the back of the car.

There is no record of what they talked about during the drive, but it is clear that they did not discuss what they should, and should not, do when they arrived at Wolf's Nick. Perhaps each of them assumed that the others knew exactly what had to be done, and that he only had to copy their actions in order to hide his own ignorance of correct procedure.

It was about one o'clock when Vasey parked by the side of the road at Wolf's Nick. While he and Johnstone went across to examine the Hudson—which, apart from a smoking rear wheel, was no longer smouldering—the three policemen, acting as individuals rather than as members of an investigating team, started a haphazard search of the area. It does not seem to have occurred to them that they had to tread softly lest they tread on some clues (and, certainly, the two Foster employees were given no instructions not to move anything in or around the car). Moreover, they apparently gave no thought to the rather elementary fact that, for building up an inferential picture of what had happened, the precise location of articles that were found could be as important as their actual discovery: either the position of such articles should have been marked before they were picked up, or the articles should have been left where they were found, perhaps with

46

some protective covering fixed over them. As it was, when one of the policemen noticed anything lying on the ground, he casually picked it up, walked across to the nearer of his colleagues, and, with some such remark as 'guess what I've found', handed the article over for inspection, comment, and further smudging of any fingerprint evidence.[8]

Perhaps because Shanks was interested in astronomy, and it was a perfect night for star-gazing, he saw nothing on the ground. Fergusson found an empty three-gill bottle, with frozen grass sticking to it, somewhere at the rear of the car; removing the stopper, he put his nose to the bottle and detected the smell of lime juice. (From a later, and probably more thorough, examination of the bottle, the conclusion was drawn that 'it smelled of lemonade and had contained no liquid that was alcoholic or inflammable'.)

Proud found two articles that were definitely associated with the crime: one was a badly burnt length of brown cloth, afterwards identified as Evelyn's scarf, which was lying 'in the ditch near the inside front wheel'; the other was her purse—open, and with a ten-shilling note protruding from it—which was discovered somewhere near the rear of the car.

Vasey had been told by Gordon Foster to find out if the Hudson was in gear, but the covering of the gear-box was too badly burnt for him to see the slots clearly, and the lever would not budge; he decided that either the car was in gear or the gear-box had melted.

After looking at various parts of the Hudson, he concluded that the fire had originated inside the car: 'the engine was scorched, but I don't think in the way it would have been had the fire started there'.

He saw that the rack for the wooden luggage box had broken away from the back of the car, and that the box itself was completely destroyed; only the steel hasp had resisted the fire. Lying on its side on the rack was an empty Shell petrol can with the cap off (the cap was discovered the following day amidst, or somewhere near, the debris of the luggage box).

When Johnstone and Rutherford had found Evelyn Foster at ten o'clock, Johnstone had noticed that the two offside doors of the car were open; now, three hours later, he saw that the front nearside door also was open—a clear indication that someone had visited Wolf's Nick in the meantime. Johnstone's observation that three doors were open at one o'clock was supported by Vasey, who stated at the inquest:

'There were certainly three doors open, but I could not swear which three. . . . When we first got there, Mr Johnstone looked at one side of the car while I looked at the other, and a nearside door was then open.' Fergusson claimed at the inquest that both the nearside doors were *closed*, but the evidence of Johnstone and Vasey, who were wholly concerned with examining the car, is far more likely to have been correct than that of the policeman, who admitted that he only 'looked around' the car. (Press photographs of the car taken the following day do not help to resolve the issue, but only show that some of the multitude of policemen who came to Wolf's Nick opened and closed the doors as often as those in a French farce. In some of the photographs, only the offside doors are open; in others, the offside doors and one or other of the nearside doors are open; in one photograph, all four doors are open, and in another, all four are shut.)

It seems incredible, but the facts lead to the conclusion that neither Shanks, Fergusson, nor Proud believed that the scene of the crime was of any real importance to the investigation. Not until two hours after the crime was reported did the police go to Wolf's Nick—and the delay would probably have been longer (indeed, one wonders if the police would have gone there at all) but for Gordon Foster's decision to send Vasey and Johnstone to look at the Hudson. The examination of the ground was cursory and haphazard, and lasted little more than a quarter of an hour. The three policemen then got back into the car that had brought them and, at Fergusson's request, Vasey drove to Kirkwhelpington before returning to Otterburn. (The reason for the detour to Kirkwhelpington does not appear in the evidence, but was probably so that Fergusson could rouse the village constable, Francis Sinton, and tell him to keep a look-out for a bowler-hatted stranger.) *Wolf's Nick was left unguarded for the rest of the night; the items that had been found—the petrol can that Vasey had pointed out to Fergusson, the bottle, the scarf, even the purse—were just left lying around.*[9]

If an anthology of nonsensical evidence were ever to be compiled, a statement by Proud at the inquest would certainly deserve inclusion. What he said was this: 'I remained on guard over the car until Constable Fergusson left to go to Kirkwhelpington.' Proud was not asked to explain what he meant by this—which was just as well for him since the statement can be construed in only two ways, one showing that he had not the faintest idea of the purpose of guarding the car, the other indicating a belief that the car needed protection from one of his own colleagues: he must have meant either that he guarded the car at the one time when it did not need guarding—or that he guarded it from Constable Fergusson.

The two Foster employees and the three policemen got back to Otterburn at about two o'clock. No other policemen had arrived in the meantime. If, during the next couple of hours, Shanks, Fergusson or Proud did anything aimed at advancing the investigation, their actions do not appear to have been recorded.

After hearing from Vasey and Johnstone about their examination of the Hudson, Gordon Foster said that they could call it a night; Tommy Rutherford was still at the garage and he, too, was told to go home. Before Johnstone and Rutherford left, Gordon reminded them that they had to be back in four hours to take the early-morning bus to Newcastle.

Evelyn Foster lost consciousness for increasingly long periods between one o'clock and half-past seven, when she died. She was unconscious at five minutes past six, when Police Inspector Edward Russell, the first senior officer to arrive at Otterburn, called at The Kennels with Fergusson, in the hope of asking her some of the questions that had been neglected during the interview at midnight.

She regained consciousness shortly before she died, and Mrs Foster spoke to her. Evelyn's eyes were completely closed by the swelling, but she slowly turned her head in the direction of her mother's voice.

'I have been murdered,' she whispered. 'Mother . . . I have been murdered.'

1  They were both farmers: James Amos ran Dyke Head Farm, William Glendenning, Cleughbrae.

2  Pronounced 'Ponteeland'.

3  At the Cockle Park meteorological station, 15 miles ENE of Wolf's Nick, the air temperature at 9 pm was 31·4°F (a little below 0°C); 14 degrees of frost were recorded in Newcastle.

4  According to his sister's recollection, 'Gordon's height was about 5ft 6in. He was not stocky but of medium build.'

5  Despite Evelyn Foster's exculpation of Primrose, he was later traced and interviewed by the police, and it was established that he was many miles away at the time.

6  In conversation with the author.

7  Since this was written, Andrew Fergusson has died.

8  At the inquest, Fergusson, when asked about fingerprints on an article discovered at Wolf's Nick, stated that evidence about fingerprints would be given by a subsequent police witness; it never was. After the inquest, the Chief Constable of Northumberland was asked if *any* articles found at Wolf's Nick were examined for fingerprints; he ignored the question.

9  The day after the inquest ended, the *Newcastle Evening Chronicle* admitted that two of its reporters visited the scene of the crime between 5 and 6 am, and 'closely examined the burnt car; opened the bonnet to discover where the fire started; and, finding Miss Foster's scarf on the ground, placed it on one of the lamps' (where it was found by the police who arrived at the scene a few hours later).

# 4

*There is nothing more stimulating than a case where everything goes against you.*

The Chief Constable of the Northumberland County Constabulary was Captain Fullarton James, OBE. A native of Kerelaw, in Ayrshire, he had retained the title of captain when, in 1897, he resigned from the Royal Scots Fusiliers to become Chief Constable of the small Welsh county of Radnor; three years later, in July 1900, when he was thirty-seven, he was appointed Chief Constable of Northumberland.

A retired policeman who joined the force soon after the Foster investigation says of Fullarton James:

'In appearance, he was the typical country gentleman-retired army officer type, and most of the time I saw him he was complete with knickerbockers and two spaniel dogs. In retrospect, many of his ideas were no doubt old-fashioned, but this was only to be expected from someone who had ruled for so long.'

This last comment is misleading for it suggests that Fullarton James's ideas *became* old-fashioned; in fact, his ideas were outdated to start with, and became antediluvian as the years went by. Except in a few relatively minor respects, the force in 1931 was no better trained or organised than at the end of the nineteenth century. The 'force orders' that Fullarton James sent out from police headquarters in the old county gaol at Morpeth usually related to existing regulations or administrative arrangements; only rarely did they announce innovations, and these were usually of the most elementary nature. For example: 'The Chief Constable's attention has been drawn to the fact that certain officers are in the habit of using their night-shift waist belt as a razor strop and directs that the practice cease.' Another of Fullarton James's orders read: 'Officers are not to accept money for payment of fines before the case is heard.'

The innovation of which he was probably most proud, and to which he seems to have given more thought than any other, was a system of coded postcards which he conceived as a cheap and confidential method of ordering individual officers to attend just about every possible variation of parade. A card marked 'Smith' meant that the officer had to parade on his bicycle in uniform, 'Jones' called him to parade on his bicycle in plain clothes, and there was even 'Robinson', which was decoded as 'parade on your bicycle in uniform for duty on foot'.

Some idea of Fullarton James's sense of priorities may be gauged from the fact that mechanised transport was first used by the force in 1923, when four motor-cycles were hired to provide an escort for the Prince of Wales on his visit to Alnwick Castle, but it was not until 1930, just a few months before the Foster case, that the force purchased its first motor vehicles—a car and four motor-cycle combinations. Whether this sudden burst of extravagance was provoked by considerations of efficiency or by rumours of another royal visit must be open to conjecture.

The reader will probably have wondered why no detectives went to Otterburn in the first hours of the Foster investigation. The explanation, simple but hard to believe, is that there *were* no detectives in the Northumberland County Constabulary. In the force of 330-odd men, there were three plain-clothes officers—stationed respectively at the relatively large towns of Gosforth, Wallsend and Blyth (Newcastle-upon-Tyne had a separate force)—but they were just police constables who were not required to wear uniform; none of them had been trained as a detective.[1] It appears that, before 1931, there was only one instance of a Northumberland policeman's using a branch of forensic science to apprehend a criminal; this was in 1926, when a constable at Ashington noticed fingerprints on some white-painted wood at the scene of a shopbreaking, and enterprisingly removed the wood and sent it to Scotland Yard with a list of suspects, one of whose set of prints was filed there and matched those on the wood.

The force was inadequate in general, let alone to the task of investigating a complex case like the death of Evelyn Foster. This was acknowledged by many people in the county, including several members of the force and all the local crime reporters. The latter, in their early accounts of the Foster case, took it for granted that if Fullarton James had not done so already, he would soon telephone the Commissioner of the Metropolitan Police to request the services of Scotland Yard officers to head the investigation. (One reporter, more daring or inventive than the rest, claimed that James Berrett, the bearded detective chief inspector who had led the investigations into two recent, much-publicised cases of murder—that of Police Constable Gutteridge in Essex in 1927 and that of the Reading tobacconist, Alfred Oliver, in 1929—was standing by, suitcase and 'murder bag' packed, to travel to Northumberland.)

But Fullarton James did not ask for assistance from Scotland Yard—did not, it seems, even consider doing so. And this despite the fact that, however chronic was his mental myopia, he must have realised that there was no one in his force capable of organising and directing a full-scale inquiry—and that without such leadership, the officers assigned to the case, untrained even in the basic routine of criminal investigation, would be like players in a game of blindman's-buff. The Foster case would not be solved except by sheer luck—by serendipity in finding a clue; by the coincidence of its being found by, or passed on to, an officer able to recognise its individual value or relevance to other information; by someone coming forward to make a criminatory statement or confession.

If Fullarton James issued a 'force order' at this time, it should have read something like:

> All officers involved in the investigation into the death of Miss Evelyn Foster are required to wear a rabbit's foot unobtrusively about their persons and to keep their fingers crossed whilst carrying out their duties.

The first policeman sent to guard the scene of the crime at Wolf's Nick arrived there from Morpeth on one of the force's new motor-cycle combinations at seven o'clock on Wednesday morning, when it was still dark. His arrival was seen by Robert Pringle, an Otterburn man who was cycling to work at Knowesgate Quarry. The air was so cold that Pringle had been unable to light the carbide lamp on his bicycle and, for fear of being charged with riding without lights, he hastily dismounted when he made out the policeman's uniform, and pushed his bike along the road. As Pringle came abreast of the burnt-out car, the policeman was already traipsing about on the moorland, every so often stamping his feet to keep them warm, with no thought of what he might be crushing underfoot. Pringle, who knew nothing of what had happened the night before, called out: 'What's up, then?'

but was told, brusquely, to 'move along'. This he did, walking with his bicycle through the 'nick' in the road, and then, being out of sight of the policeman, remounting and riding on to Knowesgate.

The policeman's lonely vigil ended soon after eight o'clock, when the sky was lightening and he was joined by other constables, who wandered around and chatted together until shortly before nine, when Inspector Edward Russell came from Otterburn and told them what he thought they should do. Russell had had the forethought to bring along a tape-measure and, assisted by a couple of the constables, he traced the tyre-marks in the heather and took some measurements to indicate the car's course across the moor:

> On the roadway I observed the marks where the car had left the road; the car had come from the west [left-hand] side of the road and gone across the road and over the embankment [which consisted of 6ft of rough stone, sloping at an angle of about 45°]. There was no sign of burning of the heather between the main road and the car. . . . The car had travelled 90 feet on falling ground, and had then turned to the left, where the wheel-marks were in a soft ditch some inches; then it continued further on. It travelled altogether 198 feet after leaving the road. I found the distance between the car and the road to be 78 feet.

As well as the articles observed the previous night by Fergusson and Proud, Russell and his helpers discovered several pieces of burnt material on the ground in the vicinity of the car. Of these, only a pair of stocking suspenders, found on the nearside, was recognisable to the naked eye.

Russell also found the cap of the Shell petrol can. This was 'lying apart' from the can, but just how far apart does not seem to have been measured; one gathers that it was no more than a foot or so from the can, which was lying among the charred remains of the wooden luggage box.

Two 'small areas' of turf appeared to be stained with blood: one was 2yd south of the car, and the other was on the north side, 4yd from the offside front wheel. (Days—perhaps weeks—later, the stains were tested to establish whether they were of blood, and the chemical reaction indicated that they were not. There seems to be no record of which of the standard preliminary tests was used, nor of whether more than one test was tried. The fact that the analyst did not attempt to identify the substance of the stains must cast doubt on his efficiency and, therefore, on his conclusion. Despite the negative finding, Inspector Russell remained convinced that the marks were of blood.)

In examining the interior of the car, Russell found a piece of burnt material on the back seat. In the cavity between the front seats, where the tools were kept, was a mass of charred paper, afterwards identified by Joseph Foster as an exercise book in which his daughter noted brief details of her hire-car transactions.

More policemen arrived at Wolf's Nick throughout the day, and though Russell seems to have tried to keep the numbers down by sending away some of the early-comers, there were times when the stretch of moorland looked more like a place of reunion than the scene of a crime. Casual sightseers were not allowed to leave the road, but no such restriction was applied to locally-exalted sightseers—magistrates, members of the Northumberland Joint Standing Committee, friends of Fullarton James—who, with their relatives and dogs, wandered freely, prodding the ground with shooting-stick or cane.

Adding to the occasional congestion, newspaper reporters and photographers vied with their respective rivals to picture the scene. Told by their editors to emphasise the loneliness of the setting, the photographers had the more difficult job, and must have needed a good deal of patience while they waited for a break in the crowd and the chance of an uncluttered shot of the car against the background of the Ottercops. For the reporters, on the other hand, the name of Wolf's Nick only had to be scribbled in their notebooks to be followed, like the automatic response in a word-association test, by purpureal phrases such as 'a pretty fold in the hills made a place of horror by the fiendish brutality of a wolf in human form'.

In the afternoon, as it was getting dark, Russell received a brief visit from Superintendent Thomas Shell who, as head of Hexham Division, was nominally in charge of the investigation. Shell told the inspector that Joseph Foster had agreed to send a breakdown lorry to tow the Hudson back to the firm's garage, and that arrangements had been made for the car to be examined at the garage by two motor engineers.

Soon after Shell's departure, a constable found a footprint in a shallow ditch a yard or so beyond the bonnet of the Hudson. Russell must have realised that it was far more likely that the mark had been made during the investigation than at the time of the crime; even so, he ordered everyone to stay away from the ditch and made a note that, the following day, a cast should be taken of the impression.

The breakdown lorry, driven by Thomas Vasey, arrived at Wolf's Nick at about half-past five. Russell agreed with Vasey that no attempt should be made to tow the car because, even if this were possible, it would probably cause further damage, which might lead to false conclusions by the examiners. A winch was used to lift the car on to the back of the lorry, and Vasey set off on the slow, six-mile journey to Otterburn.

Russell and all but one of the remaining constables left soon afterwards. The unfortunate odd-man-out, PC William Turnbull from West Woodburn, had been deputed to keep watch over Wolf's Nick—and, in particular, to guard the footprint in the ditch—until the following morning.

Throughout the day, while Russell and his men were combing Wolf's Nick, many more policemen were engaged in what the *Newcastle Evening Chronicle* described as 'the most dramatic man-hunt Northumberland has ever known'.

There was, of course, the strong possibility that the murderer was no longer in the county. The apparent sexual motive for the crime made it unlikely that the man had an accomplice, a person with a car who had collected him from Wolf's Nick. Evelyn Foster had said that, while lying on the ground, she thought she heard a car pull up and a whistle, but these sounds may have had no connection with the crime: someone driving along the road may have stopped when he saw the fire, but then, not seeing the still figure on the ground, continued on his way; what to the girl had sounded like a whistle may have been the squeal of the car's tyres on the heavily frosted road when the driver braked.

However, even on foot, the murderer would have had ample time to reach Newcastle before the hue and cry began, and either remained in the city, undistinguished and virtually undistinguishable from hundreds of men of similar appearance, or boarded a train or coach to another part of the country.

But in the early hours of Wednesday, when Superintendent Shell and other officers of Hexham Division discussed what had to be done, the question of whether or not the murderer had already escaped across the county boundary would not have received much consideration: no matter how slight its chance of success, a search had to be made.

Policemen stationed in the small towns and villages within the division were ordered to patrol local roads, keeping a look-out for a man answering this description:

Height 5ft 6in, dark, slim build and wearing bowler hat, dark (blue?) overcoat and suit.

At the same time, a message was telephoned to the superintendents of other divisional headquarters who, in turn, arranged for the roads in their respective areas to be patrolled. The description was also circulated to the headquarters of adjoining or nearby forces.

The search got under way at different times in different parts of the county, but according to press reports and interviews or correspondence with Northumbrians who journeyed to work in the early morning, few, if any, policemen were on the roads before daylight. The start of the search seems to have been delayed even in the regions of Wolf's Nick and Otterburn, let alone in those parts of the county farthest from the scene of the crime.

By about eight o'clock, however, policemen were on duty near all main cross-roads, scrutinising and questioning pedestrians, cyclists and occupants of motor vehicles. Andrew Fergusson and other constables stationed in villages on or near the road from Otterburn to Ponteland had the job of circulating the description of the wanted man to farmers and people living in outlying cottages.

The sketchiness of the description tended to emphasise one part of it —'*wearing bowler hat*'—and, almost irrespective of height and colouring, any bowler-hatted man travelling in Northumberland that day, and in the days that followed, was treated with suspicion by the police. In the early 1930s, the bowler was still a popular type of formal headgear, and even in a predominantly rural county was worn by a good many travellers—among others, farmers with business to attend to in a town, sales representatives, unemployed men wearing their Sunday-best in the hope that it would help create a good impression with possible employers. Unless such men happened to be known to the individual policemen as upright citizens, they were stopped and questioned about their movements on the Tuesday night—and if unable to give a satisfactory account, were taken to the nearest police station while inquiries were made. Anyone in a bowler who was travelling far across the county, and so passing several cross-roads, was likely to have to answer the same questions on several occasions. (One unfortunate man, a native of Darlington who had come north in search of agricultural work, was stopped half a dozen times as he trudged from farm to farm; eventually, still jobless but frightened at the prospect of being questioned yet again, he waved down a motorist who gave him a lift back to Darlington. As he was getting out of the car, he saw a police inspector and a constable standing at the roadside. 'Good God!' he cried. 'Are they here, too?' He took to his heels and quickly disappeared from sight.) The stigmatism of the bowler was increased by newspaper headlines which proclaimed MAN IN BOWLER HAT SOUGHT BY OTTERBURN INVESTIGATORS and REPORTED SIGHTING OF BOWLER-HATTED MAN, and before long men who had worn this sort of hat all their adult lives either went about bare-headed or changed to some other form of head-gear.[2]

Short of discovering the criminal in the course of the man-hunt, the best chance of identifying him seemed to lie in tracing the occupants of the car from which he had alighted at Elishaw Road Ends. On Wednesday morning, acting on Evelyn Foster's statement that the man had told her that he had met these people at Jedburgh and had tea with them there, a trio of Northumberland policemen drove to the town in a hired car and accompanied members of the local (Roxburghshire) force on a tour of hotels, restaurants and tea-shops. The tour did not take long: in the few catering establishments that remained open during the winter months, the staff had no difficulty in remembering the small number of customers in the late afternoon and early evening of the previous day; none of them recalled serving a party comprising a woman and two—or three—men.

Disappointed and not a little baffled at having drawn a blank in Jedburgh, the Northumberland policemen returned to Otterburn, breaking their journey at 'the last hotel in England', the Redesdale Arms, a mile south of Rochester and about a mile and a half before Elishaw. They probably stopped for a drink rather than in the hope of obtaining information that might assist the investigation, but in the course of conversation with the proprietor, Ben Prior, they heard about three men who had called at the hotel the night before, at about half-past six.

'They had drinks and left at about seven o'clock,' Prior said. 'They came from the north in a dark-coloured, four-seater saloon, and drove off to the south.' He thought the vehicle was an Essex (a product of the Hudson Motor Car Co, and almost identical in appearance to Evelyn Foster's hire-car); he remembered that the index mark was 'TN', showing that the car had been registered in Newcastle-upon-Tyne, and that the number consisted of four figures, the last, or last but one, being '2'. 'The men were all strangers to me,' Prior went on, 'but I did not pay any particular attention to them. They were well dressed. One might have been a squire's son, another a professional man's son, and the third might have been anything. They spoke with Scots accents. We don't get many strangers here at this time of the year, and these were the only strangers I noticed last night.'

At about the time the three policemen were talking to Ben Prior at the Redesdale Arms, one of their colleagues was at the Percy Arms in Otterburn, questioning the members of the bar staff who were on duty on the Tuesday evening. These were the landlord's daughter, Mrs Gladys Tatham, who said that she was 'in charge of the lounge all day', and John Scott, who was serving in the public bar from 6.20 until 8.20. Neither of them remembered a stranger coming in and enquiring about a lift to Newcastle or Ponteland. Asked if they had seen Evelyn Foster that evening, they both said no.

Mrs Tatham's evidence was of little value. The fact that she was in charge of the lounge did not mean that she was *in* the lounge the whole time; apart from occasional visits to replenish the fire and make sure the room was tidy, she would have entered only when one of the few guests rang the bell for service. A person could have walked in, found the room empty, and walked out again without being seen. However, if that person had been the man Evelyn Foster had driven from Elishaw, he would almost certainly have gone into the public bar —and John Scott's statement that he had not seen any strangers in the bar was strengthened by the fact that Scott had two jobs at the Percy Arms: as well as being a barman, he was the driver of the hotel's hire-car. He might have forgotten a stranger who simply came in for a drink, but he would surely have remembered if anyone had asked about getting to Newcastle or Ponteland, either by a free lift or for a fare cheaper than that quoted by Evelyn Foster.

By about mid-day on the Wednesday, after hearing of the negative results of the inquiries in Jedburgh and at the Percy Arms, Superintendent Shell must have felt that the investigation, though only a few hours old, had ground to a halt. Since daybreak, policemen had been calling on people in and around Otterburn, and taking statements from those who felt they had something helpful to say;[3] but because of transport difficulties and the lack of a 'clearing house' for information, few of the statements had been seen by Shell or his direct subordinates.

Desperately needing information that could be construed as a possible 'lead', Shell looked at Ben Prior's statement gratefully rather than critically, ignoring—or perhaps overlooking—the fact that, whereas Evelyn Foster had said that the person in the driving seat of the car at Elishaw was a woman, the visitors to the Redesdale Arms were all men. Two other points in Prior's statement raised doubts as to its relevance to the case: first, it was difficult to reconcile Evelyn's inability to identify the make of the car at Elishaw with Prior's belief that the men's car was an Essex, virtually a twin of her own Hudson; second, all three of the men who had called at the hotel spoke with a Scots accent, yet Evelyn's description of her passenger's accent was 'like Tyneside—not broad Tyneside but north-country'. (Though some southerners might confuse the accents of each side of the border, it is unlikely that Evelyn—or Prior—would have done so. One is guessing, of course, but by 'not broad Tyneside', Evelyn probably meant that the distinctive slurred 'o' of the Geordie accent—which makes the word 'overcoat' sound like 'ervercurt'—was detectable but not strong.)

Shell drove to police headquarters at Morpeth to confer with Captain Fullarton James and Superintendent James McGilvray Tough, the deputy chief constable, and this resulted in a telephone call being put through to Scotland Yard, asking for arrangements to be made for the BBC to broadcast an appeal for information on the national radio wavelength. The appeal, which was read out after the 6·15 news that night, began with a brief reference to the finding of Evelyn Foster near her burnt-out car at Wolf's Nick (with the time being given as 10·30, half an hour later than when Johnstone and Rutherford actually found her) and then gave rough descriptions of the men who had been at the Redesdale Arms and the scanty details of their car; then followed a non-sequitur—'The destination of the car is believed to be London, it having come from Scotland via Jedburgh'—and the request that 'anyone with information concerning the car or men should communicate with the Chief Constable, Northumberland, telephone number Morpeth 201, or any police station'.

Only a matter of hours after the broadcast, the driver of the car called at a police station in Doncaster, and was able to satisfy the detectives who interviewed him that neither he nor his passengers had any connection with the Foster case.

On Wednesday, the only official police statement to the press was brief and belated, issued some time after the last editions of the morning papers had been printed. Unofficially, though, in the early hours some member of the force must have telephoned a representative of the *Newcastle Chronicle* publishing group and outlined Evelyn Foster's account of how she had been attacked. The communicative policeman should have been well rewarded for this service, for it gave the group's two morning papers a scoop, with the *North Mail* printing a report of the case on its front page and the *Sporting Man* tucking a couple of paragraphs about the 'Terrible Incident Near Otterburn' amongst the tips for the day's horse and greyhound races.

The official police statement, which was printed in the local evening papers, read as follows:

> About 10 pm last night Miss Foster, of The Garage, Otterburn, was found by a bus conductor about three miles south *[sic: north-west]* of Kirk-whelpington, on the Jedburgh-Newcastle road, lying beside one of their own cars, badly burned, and the car was still burning. She was taken home to Otterburn. Will any person who may have been on that road between the hours of 7.30 and 10 pm please communicate with the police at Hexham or the Chief Constable, Morpeth?
>
> Will the party who were travelling south from Scotland in a motor-car, and from which a man whom they gave a lift alighted at Elishaw Road Ends, north of Otterburn, about 6.30 pm, kindly communicate with the police?

The conspicuous omission from the statement was Evelyn Foster's description of her assailant. By the time the statement was issued, reporters had been given the description (it was included in accounts of the case in the evening papers), but this did not explain why it was left out of the statement. The editor of the prestigious *Newcastle Daily Journal*, still smarting at being scooped by the *North Mail* and—perhaps the greater indignity—the *Sporting Man*, was further angered by the omission. He decided that the police needed a short, sharp lecture on the Power of the Press, and on Thursday published a leading article which read, in part:

> The police have a difficult task. It might have been less difficult had the newspapers been notified immediately of the crime, so that a description of the passenger in Miss Foster's car could have been circulated right throughout Northumberland and further afield. What a curious thing it is that if the police desire a dead body to be identified they will notify the Press immediately, but if it is a live body, urgently wanted for some horrible crime, they are not so quick to seek the aid of the most efficient publicity medium.

On Thursday morning, the Hudson was examined in The Garage at Otterburn by two motor engineers, William Jennings, who owned a car showroom and workshop in Morpeth, and Duncan Hodgson, the general manager of an old-established family firm of car dealers at Benton, Newcastle.

Though it seems that Hodgson, a member of the Institute of Automobile Engineers, was the more expert and that he carried out the greater part of the examination, Jennings was certainly the more talkative and willing to venture deductions from the findings. As will appear, all of Jennings's deductions were what the police hoped they would be, and one cannot help wondering if his reasoning (which, at the inquest, he was never asked to explain) was biased, perhaps unconsciously, by the fact that his place of business was just round the corner from police headquarters. Hodgson was not called at the inquest, which is a pity because his factual evidence would probably have been more detailed and comprehensive than that of Jennings—and, from what people say of his nature, he would have eschewed wild surmise.

Jennings and Hodgson made two main findings. The first was that the fire was not caused by a mechanical defect but was started by some 'outside agency' within the body of the car, probably at the rear, the flames then spreading forward; whether or not a liquid inflammable material was used, it was impossible to say.

The second finding was that the car was 'in low gear, with the engine still switched on and the hand-brake off'. The significance of the Hudson's being in gear needs to be explained—at least for the benefit of any reader who has never driven a 'veteran car'. In a modern car, standing stationary with the engine running and first gear engaged, if the driver does not either de-clutch or exert pressure with his foot on the accelerator pedal, the engine stalls. However, the Hudson Super-Six, in common with virtually all other cars of its period, was fitted with a 'hand-throttle': this was a disc at the hub of the steering wheel which, when screwed outwards, pulled on a length of piano wire which was, in turn, attached to an extension of the accelerator pedal on the engine side of the front bulkhead. A car in low gear, with the hand-brake off and the hand-throttle set at the 'fast idle' position, would travel at a constant speed and on a straight course without assistance from a driver.[4] A small obstacle or some feature of the terrain (such as the shallow ditch at Wolf's Nick where the Hudson's offside tyre tracks were found) might cause the car to alter direction, and a greater obstacle —a projecting rock, perhaps, or an upward gradient—could make the engine stall.

The fact that the Hudson was in low gear, with the engine switch on and the hand-brake off, tended to confirm what was implicit in Evelyn Foster's brief and confused account of what had happened at Wolf's Nick—that the car was driverless on its journey of 198ft from the road. Evidence on two other points could have either further confirmed or cast doubt upon this part of her statement. *First*, there was the question of whether the hand-throttle was set in the neutral or an engaged position. One or other, or both, of the motor engineers must have examined the hand-throttle, yet Jennings made no reference to it at the inquest; ignoring the possibility that he simply forgot to mention the evidence on this crucial point, the only charitable explanation for his silence is that the hand-throttle was too badly damaged for its setting to be established. *Second*, though Jennings visited Wolf's Nick and presumably searched the vicinity of where the Hudson was found, he said nothing at the inquest as to whether there was, or was not, an obstacle that might have caused the engine to stall and the car to stop where it did.

The absence of testimony on these points must mean one of two things: either that there was no evidence for Jennings to give (which is quite possible with regard to the first point, but most unlikely with regard to the second) or that he neglected to mention evidence that supported Evelyn Foster's statement. The tone of his testimony, with the inferences all pointing towards the conclusion that the girl's account of the events at Wolf's Nick bore no relation to what actually happened, rules out any likelihood that he omitted evidence that appeared to contradict her statement.

The War Memorial Hall, where the inquest was formally opened at mid-day on Thursday, was a strictly utilitarian place; the money collected for its construction had been sufficient for the bare essentials, but had not allowed for any frills of decor. White-washed walls, hemmed by a brown-stained wainscot, supported a timbered ceiling which sloped from the centre, following the lines of the roof; iron stretchers criss-crossed between the tops of the walls, spanning an uncomplicated oblong of about 30ft by 90.

At one end—the south end, farthest from the road—was a rudimentary stage, and in front of this the caretaker had placed a chair and a trestle table, covered with a strip of black cloth, for the use of Mr Philip Mark Dodds, His Majesty's Coroner for the Southern District of Northumberland. Nine chairs for the members of the jury[5] were set against the east wall, and opposite them, on the far side of the coroner's table, was a chair for witnesses. Most of the remainder of the hall's complement of chairs were spaced out in rows for the audience of reporters and spectators, and the few that were left over were placed by the west wall, near the witness chair, for the coroner's officer and policemen. The caretaker's preparations for the inquest had not included the removal of paper-chains, streamers and tinselled bunting that had been draped from the iron stretchers for a dance on the Saturday after Christmas, which Evelyn Foster had attended with George Phillipson; the decorations hung limply except when the door was opened and hastily shut against the cold, near-zero, air outside, when they lurched and flickered in the breeze.

Despite the intense interest in the case among the people of Otterburn (the blacksmith's shop, at the back of the Percy Arms, was now an unofficial information centre rather than a rendezvous for idle gossip), only one or two villagers were in the audience at the formal opening of the inquest; many others who would have liked to be there felt that, though the case was public, the tragedy was private to the Foster family, and that their attendance would seem like prying into the affairs of a neighbour. The spectators were far outnumbered by reporters; if the radio broadcast had achieved nothing, except in a negative sense, so far as the investigation was concerned, it had had the effect of spreading interest in the case beyond the boundaries of the north-eastern counties, and the local newspapermen were joined by representatives of other provincial papers and by second-string reporters for national papers who had driven the 300 miles from London overnight.

The jury entered from a small room at the back of the stage, and were followed, first, by Mr Dodds, a portly little man who had practised as a solicitor before his appointment as coroner, then by Police Constable Fergusson, who was acting as an officer of the court. The village policeman had no need to refer to his notebook as he called the names of the jurors, for each of the men was well known to him: George Mac-Dougall, the head gardener at Otterburn Tower, who was elected foreman of the jury; the Reverend Joseph Philip Basil Brierley, Vicar of Otterburn; Robert Brown and John Geddes, both of whom worked at Otterburn Mill; John Hodgson, the landlord of the Percy Arms; Stanley Potts, the sub-postmaster; George Sinclair, the manager of the village's Co-operative Store; George Waddell, the managing director of the mill; and Arthur Wallace, a local farmer.

Mr Dodds made a short speech, assuring 'the parents and the general public . . . that everything that can be done will be done to elucidate the mystery surrounding the death of Evelyn Foster', and then called the dead girl's father to give evidence of identification. This did not take more than a minute or so. As Joseph Foster waited while the coroner wrote out the deposition of his evidence, he wiped his forehead with a handkerchief—a small action that would be magnified into headlines such as STRICKEN FATHER'S ORDEAL and FATHER LABOURS UNDER GREAT EMOTION.

Without asking Joseph to return to his seat beside his son Gordon, Mr Dodds adjourned the inquest until 2 February, explaining to the jury that this was 'a formal fixing, because we may not have to meet if proceedings intervene'.

While the inquest was being opened, Stuart McDonald, Professor of Pathology at the University of Newcastle, arrived by car at The Kennels to conduct a post-mortem examination on the body of Evelyn Foster; he was accompanied by his 'technician', Albert Young, and Inspector Russell. A Scotsman, born at Castle Douglas, Kirkcudbrightshire, in 1873, McDonald had occupied the Chair at Newcastle for more than twenty years. His experience of *forensic* pathology was negligible, however, and it seems fair to assume that the coroner brought him into the Foster case, in preference to one of the police surgeons in the area, because of a feeling that, in a case that would receive much publicity, apparent eminence was more important than practical knowledge: a 'star-name' was needed to match the drama of the case, and no matter if the star was miscast.

Professor McDonald's post-mortem findings will be discussed later. Unfortunately, his notes are not available, so it is hard to assess the thoroughness of his examination. But at least one can get a rough idea of its duration from the fact that by about half-past one in the afternoon, McDonald was at Wolf's Nick, looking around with Inspector Russell, having stopped off on his way back to Newcastle.

A few feet south of where the Hudson was found, Russell chanced to see two pieces of burnt flesh (whether they were together on the ground or some distance apart, two separate discoveries by the inspector, is not clear from the evidence); he gave these to McDonald, who later examined them and concluded that one piece was 'apparently' from the palm of the hand but that it was not possible to say from which part of the body the other piece had come. Though they were worthless to the investigation, Russell's finds—at the very centre of the scene of the crime—are worth mentioning as further indications of the inefficiency of the police operations at Wolf's Nick: it is incredible—and, yes, disgraceful—that the pieces of flesh should have escaped the notice of all the dozens of men who were there, ostensibly searching, during the daylight hours of Wednesday and again on Thursday morning. In the country of the blind, the one-eyed man is king: in 1931 this, surely, would have made an excellent maxim for any Northumberland police-man ambitious for promotion.

Soon after McDonald left, William Jennings and Duncan Hodgson arrived at Wolf's Nick, each in his own car, and were shown around by Russell. When the conducted tour was over, Hodgson made some notes, then returned to his car and drove away. Jennings, however, stayed behind to hold an alfresco press conference. For the past day and a half, the reporters stationed at Wolf's Nick had had to rely wholly on their powers of description; now, at last, they were presented with some bright, indeed gaudy, quotes to enliven their accounts. As befitted a motor engineer, Jennings started his discourse in low gear, referring to facts which the reporters had already observed for themselves regarding the terrain and the path the Hudson had taken; then, impelled by the flattery of fascinated faces, he mentioned facts only in order to draw conclusions from them.

'It seems that the car pulled up on the left-hand side of the road from Belsay to Otterburn,' he said. 'Apparently it was restarted, and went over the embankment, with the driving wheel locked to the right.'

Now came the first public questioning of a part of Evelyn Foster's statement:

'I think there was someone at the wheel, because the car was righted after it had crossed a ditch thirty yards from where it went over the embankment. There are no traces of fire in its tracks, which suggests that it was set on fire after it had stopped.'

Probably because the press at this time had only an incomplete version of Evelyn Foster's statement, made up of scraps of information from diverse sources, the significance of Jennings's last remarks was not appreciated. They were included in accounts that appeared that night and the next morning, but near the end and without either comment or typographic emphasis.

For an hour or so after Jennings had gone, the reporters at Wolf's Nick sat huddled in their cars, with the windows closed and the engines running so as to provide a little warmth, and dozed or stared unhopefully at the perambulating policemen, who by now seemed as appropriate to the landscape as the black-faced sheep they had temporarily supplanted. Then, late in the afternoon, the reporters witnessed one of the least explicable episodes of the investigation. Superintendent Tough and three other officers arrived from Morpeth in the constabulary car and proceeded to the spot where a footprint had been found the day before. This discovery had been considered sufficiently important to be guarded during the night, but after taking only a cursory look at the impression, Tough and his men turned their backs on it and walked about ten yards away to examine another part of the ground; one of the officers then chiselled out two slices of turf which presumably also carried footprints. These were put in the side-car of a police motor-cycle, and the driver set off towards Otterburn, his probable destination being Andrew Fergusson's cottage. Then, as noted by the reporter for the *Evening World*:

Apparatus consisting of a saucepan and a spirit stove was erected near the first footprint, but after a conference it was packed up again and the officers left shortly afterwards. Superintendent Tough declined to reveal the nature of the work they were engaged upon.

The footprint that had been guarded during the night can only have been discarded as a possible clue because either it had clearly been made some time before the crime or it bore characteristic marks of a police regulation boot. One of these alternatives may also explain why the police never revealed the results of the examination of the pieces of turf that were taken away.[6]

By Friday, the investigation had run out of steam. Perhaps as much to create an impression of activity as because of a belief that the murderer was still hiding in the area, the police responded to every report, no matter how tenuous or vague, of a stranger being sighted in some out-of-the-way place.

As the result of one of these reports, a man was discovered on the fells north of Knowesgate, six or seven miles from Wolf's Nick. According to the *Newcastle Evening Chronicle*, 'He was carrying a bowler hat, and the fact that he was not wearing it led the police to the conclusion that he was endeavouring to hide it.' The man was taken to Belsay police station, where he explained that he had lost his job two days before and, being afraid to go home, had tramped the moors, sleeping in the open at night; he said that he had written to his family, telling them that he was not coming back. After being detained for several hours, while the police contacted his former employer and confirmed that his family had received the letter, he was allowed to leave. It would be nice to know if he then decided to go home, feeling that his family's wrath held no terrors after his experiences on the moors and in a police interview room, but there appears to be no information on this point.

Then there was the incident, casting doubt on the validity of a famous Holmesian deduction, of the dog that did not bark in the night. Constable Fergusson was called to a farm near Otterburn, and there, in a cow byre, he found a man sleeping in the straw alongside the farm's watch-dog. The dog had taken a fancy to its sleeping-companion, and when Fergusson and the farmer approached, it became quite ferociously protective towards the man; no amount of cajolery by the farmer or truncheon-waving by Fergusson would make the dog budge. The assortment of sounds—the dog's growling, the farmer's lip-pursing, Fergusson's cursing—eventually woke the man; thinking that the dog and the policeman were allies, he began whimpering with fear, and this new sound apparently caused such uneasiness in the animal that it felt constrained to lope out of the byre and relieve itself. The man was only too happy for Fergusson to take him to the police house, and on the way he admitted that he was a deserter from the Royal Scots; he said that he had hitch-hiked from his barracks at Tidworth in Wiltshire to Ferryhill in County Durham, and there 'misappropriated' a bicycle and ridden the 50 miles to Otterburn. Inquiries by the military police established that the soldier had deserted after 6 January, and he was escorted back to Tidworth to face court-martial.

The report that led to perhaps the greatest expenditure of police time and energy came from a shepherd—a 'sentinel of the hills,' as at least two papers described him—who said that he had seen a man answering the murderer's description walking on Bogswood Moor, about 15 miles west of Otterburn. It was certainly odd that anyone unconnected with sheep should have taken a mid-winter stroll on Bogswood Moor, a place as uninviting as its name suggests, and the police spent two days combing the moor and the area round about, in the hope of either tracing the man or finding evidence to show that the shepherd had not seen some sort of marshland mirage. Having drawn a blank, they again interviewed the shepherd, who by now had recalled a few details to add to his earlier description of a man 'who looked as though he had just come from a city': for instance, that he was carrying a bulky canvas pack, that he was wearing a tweed cap and thin yellow shoes, and that, despite the bitter weather, he had his overcoat flung over his shoulder. These details, none of them the least urban and none of them supporting the shepherd's assertion that 'the man looked exactly like the description given by the dying girl'—may have made the police ask themselves if they had been chasing a very wild goose indeed; anyway, the search was called off.

These episodes are merely illustrative; there were dozens more police searches sparked off by sightings of strangers, some bowler-hatted, some not. With little else to report, yet needing to fill at least a column beneath the front-page headlines on the case, the press tended to 'write up' the searches; several accounts carried headlines of the STARTLING-NEW-EVIDENCE sort but contained nothing but a string of rhetorical vignettes of constables looking in barns, prodding bundles of straw, or simply standing on high ground and surveying the landscape. In and around Otterburn, the newspapers' artificial emphasis on the searches joined with rumours and created a fresh one—that the police had a strong reason for thinking that the murderer was still in the district. As the days passed, as the reports of the searches continued but no arrest was made, a feeling of uneasiness was strengthened into one of fear; an old Northumberland saying, 'hunger brings the fox to the farm', acquired a fresh currency.

Having, albeit unintentionally, played a major part in creating the fear, the press then made matters worse by concocting stories from the fear itself. TERROR GRIPS MOORLAND VILLAGES was the kind of headline that began to appear during the first weekend of the investigation, and the following, from the *Newcastle Daily Journal*, gives an idea of the tenor of the accounts:

> It is significant that much of the police activity is centred on scouring the district, and shepherds and farm workers have been asked to keep a sharp look-out for anything that will assist in tracing the assailant.
> I find that among the country folk themselves there is a strong belief that the assailant is still at large in the district, although they do not believe he is a local man. They say there is no reason why, even in this cold weather, a man may not hide for days in the many shelters and 'hemmels' which abound in the moorlands.
> As one weather-beaten shepherd pointed out, even an aeroplane was lost in that district for many days before search parties found it. In any case, there is a most uneasy feeling throughout the area, and cottage doors are being more securely bolted than ever. Last night a motor-cyclist, seeking assistance, had the utmost difficulty in getting a cottager to open his door.

While many people locked themselves in, those who had to be out at night took precautions against attack. Cecil Johnstone recalls that after doing 'late turns' in his bus with Tommy Rutherford, he carried a heavy stick—a 'clout'—as he walked to his home, which was some way outside Otterburn. (Johnstone felt that he had a particular reason for trepidation. A day or so after the crime, he received an oddly-worded postcard, posted locally, which he thought might have come from the murderer or an accomplice; he handed the card to the police, and cannot now remember the message.)

That the fear extended across the border is shewn by the recollection of Mrs Margaret Scott, who was then thirty-one and living in the village of Minto, near Hawick:

> I blacked out all my windows and had a chopping axe and bread knife

under my pillow as my husband was working away from home. A day or so after Miss Evelyn Foster met her death, a well-dressed man with white hands came walking into Minto and asked for work. Everybody said this man was the wanted man. The schoolmaster got him to cut logs and then he went on his way, but it was a fearful scare at the time—everybody was scared, not just me.

After about a week, however, the fear began to evaporate—first, it seems, among the people who lived in the most out-of-the-way places, then in the villages, lingering longest in Otterburn, where it was kindled both by the sight and sound of policemen setting off on new search expeditions and by the rumours, one far stronger than the rest, that the murderer was being sheltered by a local person. Justifying their vanished or vanishing fears, people asserted that the murderer *had* been hiding in the area but was now dead. The first reporter to catch this story was the man on the *Evening Chronicle*, who, on 13 January, used the elementary but potent poetry of place-names to elongate the bare theory into several inches of column-space. Beginning with the unarguable facts that 'bitter winter weather has prevailed in the wilds of Northumberland since the Otterburn murder, and today the country-side was mantled with snow,' he went on to pose a question and filigree a possible answer:

Has the murderer of Evelyn Foster perished in the wild fells?
During the past few days I have practically circled this grim North-West corner of England, where main roads are few and far between. Time and time again I have traversed wild moorland roads in search of some clue of a wandering stranger endeavouring to evade the widespread net of the law.
Never before have I realised that within 50 miles of industrial Tyneside lies one of the wildest and most desolate areas in Great Britain, and the uncannily confident belief is very strongly held among the hill folk on both sides of the border that the Otterburn murderer has penetrated into this treacherous maze, lost his way in the descending mists at nightfall, completely vanished from the ken of man, and died of exposure in some hiding place miles from human habitation. . . .
Right up the Otterburn road, over Carter Bar, along the Jedburgh-Riccarton trail, which runs parallel to the border, and away down the line to Keilder and Plashetts and Falstone, the grim news has travelled.
It is known up Hunter's Burn, and the wild Loaning Burn; it is whispered up the Kennel Burn, along the Keilder Burn, even as far as the Curry Burn, which tumbles from its source in the girdle stone.
Even it has reached the craggy stream of Dead Water, and the Dead Water may hold the grim secret of the mystery of the Moors.

The shrewd country folk, who know the treacherous nature of this countryside in winter, point out that a fugitive from justice endeavouring to avoid detection can lose his way or perish among the crags.

Many with whom I have talked have confidently predicted that the murderer's body will be found in the circle of mountains and crags bordered by Carter Fell, Ellis Crag, Emblehope Cairn, Round Raw, Monkside, Peel Fell, and the Girdle Stone.

It may be days or weeks or even months before the body is found, but they feel confident that the wild Northumberland moors have claimed both murderer and his victim.

From early in the morning on Sunday, 11 January, a day of mist and sleety rain, hundreds of people arrived in Otterburn to attend or, in most cases, simply to witness Evelyn Foster's funeral. Many of them came on foot from villages and farms within a radius of some ten miles; others, chiefly from farther afield, came in cars or buses (but not Foster buses, for Joseph Foster had suspended services so that all his employees could be there); a number of farmers came on horseback or, with their families, in horse-drawn wagons, and the Dowager Lady Redesdale was driven to the church in her brougham, with the horse caparisoned in black.

At two o'clock, the coffin was borne from The Kennels to St John's by four Foster employees, and was followed by members of the family, then by a throng of friends—among them, George Phillipson—walking ten or fifteen abreast, filling the street. The cortege was met by Vicar Brierley; behind him, hovering discreetly, was George MacDougall, the Vicar's Church Warden[7] and a fellow-member of the jury that would decide how Evelyn Foster met her death.

The church was soon filled, and as the service began, crowds of people, far more than were inside, stood in the churchyard and in the road, listening to the muted strains of the organ, played by Miss Ferry, the schoolmistress. As the hymn, *Rock of Ages*, was heard, women and children, and even some of the men, began to weep. Henry Adams, who stood with his parents in the road, recalls 'the sound of the organ, all around me people sobbing, others repeating the words of the hymn, and over all the splashing of the rain—there were all these sounds, but what seemed the loudest sound of all was the silence, a special sort of silence that seemed to enclose the village and keep it separate from anywhere else in the world'.

It was raining heavily when the coffin was brought out, but the men in the crowd stood bare-headed until the grave, just to the right of the lich-gate, was filled and banked with wreaths and bunches of flowers. Mrs Foster was crying as, supported by her husband and son, she walked back to the house, the crowd parting in front of her to form what one reporter called 'an avenue of sorrow'. Still the crowd was silent; there was sympathy for the family, and many of the people felt grief, but the feelings were apparent enough not to require words as the Fosters passed.

The funeral entailed additional duties for the police. As well as the constables who diverted traffic north and south of the village—at Elishaw and at the side-road by the mill—several policemen in plain clothes mingled with the crowd, presumably because their superiors hoped that if there was anything in the saying that a murderer always returns to the scene of his crime, then the murderer of Evelyn Foster might be so obliging as to vary the practice by being present at his victim's funeral. But whereas none of the policemen noticed anyone disfigured in a way that even remotely resembled the mark of Cain, they themselves were so unused to working in their Sunday-best as to be easily recognised as sham mourners by several people in the crowd. It is said that one was reported to another for acting in a suspicious manner, but this may be the remnant of a story concocted in the village against the police.

There were a good many stories of this sort. Their incidence, and their circulation, increased as the investigation wore on and as an anti-police, 'them-and-us' feeling developed among the people of Otterburn. The first stories—amused and sometimes amusing, with only an undercurrent of bitterness—reflected oddities of police behaviour; but later, when it seemed that an attempt was to be made, not to pass the buck, but to pretend that there was no buck to pass, the stories became instruments of anger.

One of the early stories concerned the police's occupancy of certain ground-floor apartments at Otterburn Tower as 'murder headquarters'. With the permission of the owner, Mrs Howard Pease, who was away in London, the police moved in during the first weekend of the investigation, and the story was soon going the rounds that they had such poor sense of direction that George MacDougall, the gardener and only full-time member of Mrs Pease's staff, was often called upon to lead search parties to find officers who had strayed into the far reaches of the mansion and been unable to find their way back.

In the oak-panelled, chandeliered splendour of Otterburn Tower, the police had the chance to bring together, collate and assess the relevance of the diverse information collected during the first three or four days, and to combine it with later reports and statements. (As will be seen, whether they did this—or rather, whether they did it with objective efficiency—is open to question.)

As well as the information that was received direct by the Northumberland County Constabulary, a number of reports were passed on to them from other police forces. Two of these reports—perhaps more—were of men who had walked into police stations and confessed to the murder, but had turned out to have no connection with the crime. Volunteers of this sort, seeking either notoriety, a vicarious involvement in a sensational case, or even a gallows method of suicide, were —and, to a lesser extent since the abolition of capital punishment, still are—common in murder investigations; indeed, some forces kept a 'tendency list' of the names of people who had acquired a confessional habit.

The various public appeals for information, most of which were directed towards tracing the woman-driver of the car at Elishaw, produced a flood of letters and of telephone calls. But almost all these communications ignored the specific questions in the appeals, and instead put forward theories or. offered general advice; one or two people used the appeals as an excuse to complain about neighbours or relatives against whom they held a grudge, and there were, of course, the usual offers of help from astrologers, spirit-mediums, clairvoyants, water-diviners, owners of blood-hounds, and avid readers of Freeman Wills Crofts.

The Fosters, too, received several hundred letters. Most of these were expressions of sympathy, but there was a small number, invariably anonymous and often larded with quotations from the scriptures, that abused the parents for having allowed Evelyn to drive unchaperoned at night. Even more viciously, a few anonymous letters accused the family, or some member of it, of being in league with the murderer, having in some way induced him to commit the crime on their behalf; in these letters, if a motive was asserted, it usually had something to do with insurance. Some of these correspondents considered it suspiciously unmaternal that, when Evelyn was brought back from Wolf's Nick, Mrs Foster, rather than rushing to the bus, had run upstairs to prepare the bed; contrarily, others suggested that Joseph's 'display of emotion' at the opening of the inquest was no more than skin-deep, a subtly contrived imitation of sorrow. After the arrival of the first of these 'torturers' letters', as Dorothy Foster describes them, Gordon took it upon himself to protect his parents' feelings by monitoring the mail, letting them see only the messages of sympathy and forwarding the abusive or accusative letters to the police, together with those containing theories or information regarding the case.

Of the fifty or so letters of the latter type, the Fosters were aware of only one which at all interested the police. This came from a man in Bellingham, and was a long and rambling dissertation on aspects of the investigation. What intrigued the police was that certain facts mentioned in the letter had not been referred to in newspaper accounts and were believed by the police to be known only to themselves. The Fosters agreed to invite the man to The Kennels, and he arrived one Sunday at tea-time. Extraordinarily tall, his speech disjointed, as were his movements, he talked continuously for about an hour, then abruptly said goodbye. Long before he left, however, it was clear that his knowledge of the case, though wide, was also shallow, and the family decided that the police would be wasting their time in interviewing him. Margaret Foster's estimation that he was 'a very odd gentleman' was confirmed a few months later, when he was arrested on a charge involving transvestism.

Still, his oddness does not explain how he came by, as it were, privileged information. Leaving aside inspired guesswork (although, without knowing the nature of the information and, therefore, whether or not it might have been inferred from the published facts, this must remain a possibility), the most likely explanation is that he learnt the facts from the police—either directly, in conversation with a member of the force, or by eavesdropping on police shop-talk, perhaps in a Bellingham pub or café. (In Otterburn itself, several policemen became temporary regulars at the Percy Arms, and some of the many rumours seem to have stemmed from overheard—or misheard—snatches of their conversation.)

The breaches of police security were individually minor compared with a number of 'leaks' of information to the press which look suspiciously intentional—as if their aim was to affect public opinion on how Evelyn Foster met her death. These leaks reached a wide audience, for though some of the local papers—notably, the *Newcastle Daily Journal*—refrained from publishing such information, in criticising their rivals for doing so, they obliquely drew attention to it. Perhaps the most blatant example of leaked information was that which led to reports that certain of Professor McDonald's post-mortem findings did not accord with the dead girl's statement; the information was said to have come from a 'reliable source', but from all one can gather, McDonald was an exemplar of circumspection and a strict disciplinarian, so it seems most improbable that the leak sprang from the Department of Pathology in the University of Newcastle.

The journalist most favoured with titbits of illicit information was Leslie Randall of the *Daily Express*, several of whose reports, read with the benefit of hindsight, appear to be propaganda for what was sub-sequently revealed as the police's solution to the mystery of Wolf's Nick. Something that happened following the announcement of the inquest jury's verdict (and which will be mentioned when that point in the story is reached) makes one wonder whether the 'high-ranking police officer' who fed Randall with information was, in fact, the *highest-*ranking policeman in the county—Captain Fullarton James, the Chief Constable.

From the end of the first week of the investigation until the opening of the inquest, the local papers on most days managed to find something to say about the Foster case; but many of the reports relied heavily, if not wholly, on journalistic ingenuity. On days when there was little or no real news to meet the public demand, editors tended to let neces-sity be the mother of invention. Thus, a report that on the day after the crime a stranger had bought a packet of cigarettes from a shop in an unidentified village was invested with spurious 'news-value' by the comment that 'the man the police are looking for is, on a statement of Miss Foster, an inveterate smoker'.

The best example of how certain sections of the press turned an acorn of dubious information into a forest of words is 'the American suspect' who substituted for real news round about 15 January. It was reported that the Liverpool police were searching for this man (what was not reported was the rather salient fact that the search was on behalf of the American Consulate, whom the man had asked for assistance in finding a ship on which to work his passage home); he had been in Britain for about two months, and some time or other had paid a fleeting visit to Newcastle. These sparse facts were elongated into dozens of column-inches. One specially audacious report started off by talking about a 'most interesting development', then proceeded to give negative answers to the question posed in the headline, DID AMERICAN FIGURE IN TRAGEDY?, first by stating that the Northumberland police had no interest in the Liverpool inquiry, second, by quoting Joseph Foster as saying that his daughter could hardly have failed to recognise an American accent. Determined to keep a spark of life in the story, the reporter sought to counter Joseph's unhelpful reaction by commenting: 'It does not necessarily follow, however, that Miss Foster's assailant, if an American, had a well-defined American accent.' By various journalistic forms of artificial respiration, the story was kept alive through several editions, then obituarised in a single, unobtrusively-situated sentence: 'The police have satisfied themselves that the citizen of the United States mentioned in connection with the case was not associated in any way with the moorland tragedy.'

A sifting of the newspaper reports leaves no more than two or three that describe incidents of any lasting interest, let alone importance:

*Item.* On Friday, 16 January, more than a week after the guard had been removed, the police returned to Wolf's Nick. That a deal of importance was attached to the visit is indicated by the presence in the contingent of every one of the leaders of the investigation. Even Captain Fullarton James turned up; Superintendent Shell, the titular head of the investigation, was there, and so were Superintendent Spratt of Alnwick, Inspector Russell and Constable Fergusson. (Though the latter was of lowly rank, it seems fair to refer to him as a leader of the investigation because of his ubiquity. He played a part in virtually every aspect of the case, and his name crops up in newspaper reports more often than those of all the senior officers put together.) The visit, as well as being oddly timed in the sense of belatedness, was ill-timed as far as the weather was concerned. The *Newcastle Evening Chronicle* reporter wrote:

> With a gale of wind making their coat tails blow open, and with drenching rain lashing their faces, the police officials carefully dug out the scorched turf without damaging it, and placed it piece by piece in wooden boxes. They cut away all the turf on which the car had stood ['a rectangle,

10 feet by 8 feet,' according to another account], and some around it, including where Miss Foster was found lying burned. The turf was taken away in a lorry.

For proponents of 'learning by doing' and 'on-the-job training', the Foster case seems to provide only one example they might cite to back their claims. At the start of the investigation, hardly any of those involved thought of marking the position of objects that were moved—but before the sod-cutting began, measurements and notes were taken by a member of the Northumberland County Council Surveyor's Department, then each piece of turf was placed in a numbered bag and a correspondingly numbered peg hammered into the ground.

The reporter for the *Newcastle Daily Journal* found it 'somewhat strange' that the turf had not been removed before. He tried, not at all successfully, to imagine what Professor McDonald, the recipient of the turf, hoped to find in it after a week in which it had started off frozen solid, had then thawed, and at the end had been waterlogged by heavy rainstorms: a week, too, in which it had been trodden by countless feet —police feet during the first couple of days, and afterwards, especially over the weekend, the feet of scores of sightseers. (One of the jokes circulated in Otterburn was to the effect that if grapes rather than heather had been indigenous to Wolf's Nick, the police could have had a Bacchanalian orgy.) The *Journal* reporter's puzzlement appears never to have been resolved; presumably, the turf was microscopically examined, and parts of it analysed, but the results of these labours were not mentioned by Professor McDonald in his evidence at the inquest.

*Item.* The one thing that seemed clear about what happened at Wolf's Nick on the night of 6 January was that all the burns on Evelyn Foster's body were caused by petrol being thrown over her and ignited. But during the second week of the investigation, even this conclusion was questioned, for according to the reporter for the *Newcastle Evening Chronicle:*

A startling new theory that vitriol was thrown over Miss Evelyn Foster before she met her tragic death on the lonely Otterburn moorlands now confronts the police, who confess themselves baffled by the extraordinary turns which events have taken. Two facts support that theory. . . .
The coat in which Mr Cecil Johnstone, the bus driver, wrapped Miss Foster when he found her dying beside the burning car shows signs of

78

having been burnt with acid. Then Mr Foster, Evelyn's father, told me that the blankets on the bed into which the dying girl was put when she was brought home were similarly burnt.

The police did not remain baffled for long. A spokesman at the headquarters in Morpeth told the *Chronicles*'s rival, the *Evening World*, that the story was 'all wrong. We have had no information whatever about corrosive acid.'

This peremptory rebuttal seems to have stifled further comment on the vitriol theory. Still, it would be interesting to know just what the spokesman meant: the fact that the police had no information does not necessarily mean that there was none. Was the story put to a metaphorical acid test; were the coat and blankets subjected to a literal one? If the answer in both cases is yes, there remains the question of how Cecil Johnstone and Joseph Foster could have confused transferred marks of burns with actual burning. No explanation was given at the time; and now, after so many years, it is unlikely that the mystery—seemingly small but perhaps vital to an understanding of the Foster case—can be cleared up.

*Item.* Joseph Foster was again in the news on 21 January, when it was reported that he had proposed to the police that a reward be offered for information from the 'mystery woman in the case'—she who, according to Evelyn's statement, had been in the driver's seat of the car at Elishaw. Gordon Foster told reporters:

> If the police favour the proposal, my father will be prepared to pay a substantial amount, because we believe that woman can give information to the police which will result in my sister's assailant being traced. On the other hand, if for any reason the police do not agree with the proposal, my father will be satisfied that they are doing their utmost in their own way to trace the woman. It is strange that after a fortnight of repeated appeals, the woman has not come forward.

The reporter for the *Newcastle Daily Journal* pointed out that there were any number of 'possible reasons for the lady's reticence—none of them connected with the Otterburn tragedy at all':

> There may be private reasons for hiding an indiscretion; there may be the possibility of someone having a car out without authority of an employer; there may be many reasons which make a driver hesitate to come forward and say where he or she was on a certain evening, and none of them may be criminal.
> I have grounds for saying that any such reason need not be a deterrent to

coming forward. The police are more anxious to investigate Evelyn Foster's death than to be inquisitors of the private affairs of a kindly-disposed motorist who may have unwittingly carried the man who holds the secret of the Wolf's Nick tragedy.

This guarantee by proxy, which also appeared in other newspapers, had no effect. The woman, if she existed and had done nothing criminal, evidently decided that the security of silence was more attractive than an unofficial, and therefore unreliable, assurance of anonymity.

Joseph Foster's suggestion of a reward was turned down by the police. If they gave a reason, it was almost certainly not the true one. By now, Captain Fullarton James and the senior officers on the case had convinced themselves that the woman in the car—indeed, the whole episode at Elishaw—was a figment of Evelyn Foster's imagination. The obvious corollary was that the girl's story of what had happened on the road between Otterburn and Belsay, and at Wolf's Nick, was a pack of lies from beginning to end. The woman did not exist—ergo, neither did the man. And vice versa. It was all very logical; as arithmetically simple as one minus one.

As 2 February, the date of the resumed inquest, drew near, the investigation became, as it were, a two-storey structure. The lower ranks plodded on as before—conducting house-to-house, farm-to-farm inquiries, checking the records of men and officers, in that order, at the Redesdale army camp, following up belated reports of strangers being sighted—but at Otterburn Tower and at police headquarters, the leaders of the investigation searched among reports and statements, not for information that might lead to a murderer, but for information that might go towards bolstering the theory that no murder had been committed.

The inquest would be, in effect, a trial. Perhaps uniquely, a woman would be accused of having invented her own murder. If a few of the officers closest to Captain Fullarton James were not wholly confident of the outcome, he himself refused to entertain the slightest doubt that the inquest jury's verdict would be the one he wanted, needed: Evelyn Foster would be found guilty of the ultimate lie.

1 Captain Fullarton James retired on 5 September 1935, and one of the first actions of his successor, Captain Henry Studdy, was to set up a criminal investigation department.

2 It would not be surprising if the Foster case caused a slump in the sale of bowlers in Northumberland in January 1931. If it did, the case could be tenuously linked with two nineteenth-century cases with sartorial side-effects. In 1849, Maria Manning, convicted with her husband of murdering Patrick O'Connor, wore black satin for her final appearance in public, on the scaffold outside Horesemonger Lane Gaol, and this put an end to the vogue for such material. On the other hand, the fashion for low-crowned toppers seems to have been reinforced when, in 1864, Franz Müller committed the first murder on an English train and, after mistakenly picking up his victim's hat instead of his own, abbreviated it to a style that for a time bore the name of the 'Müller hat'.

3 To avoid repetition, the evidence of people who gave statements that were considered important by the police will be presented in the next chapter; certain other statements will be discussed in the chapter that follows.

4 Donald Godwin Morris, a car enthusiast of Hilton, Derby, recalls: 'When I was a boy, my father had a Hudson Super-Six. We lived in Worcestershire at the time, about 1929–30, and frequently made a journey along a gated road. My father would stop the Hudson a few yards from the gate, half-apply the handbrake, select low gear and set the hand-throttle. He would then get out of the car, open the gate and wait whilst the 'big six' idled its way past him. He would then close the gate and walk after the car and regain the driving seat. I know that it sounds dangerous in this day and age, but this performance was carried out more times than I can remember. The gated road is still gated; it is called Otherton Lane and is near Worcester.'

5 The number of jurors at an inquest is not less than seven and not more than eleven.

6 In weighing the likelihood of whether *any* footprints at Wolf's Nick—found by the police or not—could have been connected with the crime, one is not helped by press assessments of the state of the ground: the reporter for the *Newcastle Daily Journal* asserted that 'anyone who traversed that iron-bound ground, solid with days of frost, would find it hard to believe that any footprint was of recent origin,—yet the reporter for the *Northern Echo* claimed that the footprint found on the Wednesday 'was in ground that had been softened by the water from a ditch'.

7 At that time, the vicar appointed one warden and the congregation another, the latter being known as the People's Warden.

## 5

*How often have I said to you that when you have eliminated the impossible, whatever remains, however improbable, must be the truth?*

**Monday, 2 February**

The Christmas decorations had been taken down in the War Memorial Hall. When, promptly at half-past ten, Philip Dodds, the coroner, took his place at the black-draped table in front of the stage, the hall was crowded; there were more people than there were chairs, and some of the late arrivals had to stand near the entrance door. Captain Fullarton James sat with geometrical precision in one of the reserved seats near the front, his back exactly vertical, his lap making a perfectly horizontal surface for his hat, baton, and gloves, palm-to-palm as if in prayer. He was flanked by a dozen or so of his senior officers, including the Deputy Chief Constable, Superintendent Tough, all of them striving to emulate his angularity and immobility.

That the inquest was to be as much a contest as an inquiry was indicated by the presence of two Newcastle solicitors: Thomas Hedley Smirk, representing the police, and Ernest Bates, who attended on behalf of the Foster family.

Before calling the first witness, Mrs Foster, the coroner warned the jury that statements made by Evelyn when she returned from Rochester and, later, after she had been brought back from Wolf's Nick, were not to be accepted as evidence of fact: 'You will have to take them as part of the inquiry, and see whether the evidence, direct or circumstantial, confirms them.' This was a necessary caveat but, coming at the very start of the proceedings, it scored a point for the police; in many minds, it must have been translated to mean that Evelyn Foster was to be considered guilty of lying until proved innocent.

Mrs Foster made an excellent witness. Her recollection of most of what her daughter had said was clear and detailed—often the actual

82

words rather than a rendering of them; when she was at all unsure, she said so. Her evidence must have had a profound effect on almost everyone in the hall, seeming to recreate the scenes at The Kennels on the night of 6 January, seeming to bring the dead girl to life again.

In answer to the coroner's final question, 'Did your daughter have any worries?', Mrs Foster replied: 'None, as far as I know.'

Then it was Mr Smirk's turn to examine the witness. After assuring her that anything he asked would be 'for the sole purpose of assisting the inquiry', he asked if she knew—'of her own knowledge'—whether Evelyn had called at the Percy Arms for the man, a question that was wholly inappropriate to the witness and whose sole purpose was to establish the police theory that the man did not exist. How could Mrs Foster, at The Kennels, have had 'her own knowledge' of what happened at the Percy Arms, nearly a quarter of a mile away? If, instead of answering no to the question, as she did, she had mentioned something she had been told, Mr Smirk would have pointed out that this was not 'her own knowledge'—and would have done so in such a way as to imply that she was seeking an escape from a question she did not wish to answer. (Later in the day, the two people fitted to give evidence about callers at the Percy Arms—Gladys Tatham, the landlord's daughter, and John Scott, the barman—both said that they had seen neither a stranger nor Evelyn Foster that Tuesday night.)

Mr Smirk's next questions were aimed at highlighting what appeared to the police to be a suspicious dichotomy between Evelyn's promise to her mother that she would get George Phillipson to accompany her on the drive to Ponteland and the fact that she had not done so. Encouraged by Mrs Foster's agreement that her daughter Margaret had seen Phillipson in the village soon after Evelyn left, Mr Smirk ventured further, eliciting from the witness that, after Evelyn was brought back from Wolf's Nick, her only explanation as to why she had travelled alone with the stranger was that she had not seen Phillipson as she was driving to the Percy Arms and 'had not troubled' to call at the bothie where he stayed with other Foster employees whose homes were outside Otterburn.

Mr Smirk's satisfaction was diminished, however, when Mrs Foster added conjecture to her answer: 'Since then, I've thought that my daughter did not care about going to his [Phillipson's] lodgings.' This suggestion may well have impressed the members of the jury, who thought of the bothie more as a doss-house than as 'lodgings', and knew that some of the occupants, having submitted to Gordon Foster's discipline during the day, were unrestrained in manner and speech at night; fights had occurred in the bothie, and on one or two occasions Joseph had had to deal with complaints from people living nearby of shouting and cursing. A woman less shy than Evelyn Foster would have thought twice before calling at the bothie—especially when the reason was to ask her boy-friend to act as chaperon, thus providing an obvious cue for impromptu jokes about them both.

Mr Smirk ended the examination with a couple of nervously euphemistic questions concerning Evelyn's menstrual period:

'You understand to what I refer when I speak of the "normal indisposition" of a young woman? When did this last occur with your daughter?'

'Normally, it would have been on 21 December.'

'Could she have been "unwell" on 6 January?'

'No, not as far as I know.'

One wonders if Mr Smirk was so delicate, so circumspect, with these questions that the all-male jury was befogged by his reason for asking them, which must have had something to do with the theory that women are more likely to be involved in accidents, attempt to commit suicide, or behave aggressively, even criminally, during the premenstrual period or during menstruation than at other times.[1]

When Mr Smirk sat down, the coroner asked Mrs Foster to identify the blackened remnants of Evelyn's clothing. She nodded to show that she recognised them, then burst into tears and seemed about to collapse. A constable brought her a glass of water; then, at the coroner's request, Mrs Christian Jennings, her neighbour, started to assist her from the hall. Mrs Foster indicated that she wanted to stay, however, and resumed her seat between Joseph and Gordon.

The next two witnesses were bus drivers. John Robson, a Foster employee, said that he was on the Newcastle-Otterburn run in the early evening of 6 January; he reached Raylees Farm, roughly two miles from Otterburn, 'at about 7.22', and saw Evelyn's Hudson travelling in the opposite direction: 'it was going very slowly—not more than ten miles an hour. . . . Owing to the headlights, I could not see who was in the car.'

The second driver, Robert Harrison, was employed, not by Foster's but by another Northumberland bus firm, Tait & Co. His evidence was that he left Knowesgate for Newcastle 'at about 7.30 pm' and that he 'passed nothing travelling north [that is towards Otterburn—or, more to the point, Wolf's Nick] between there and Belsay'—where, according to Evelyn Foster's statement, the man forced her to reverse the car and drive back.

A simple piece of arithmetic shows that Harrison was a quite irrelevant witness. The only apparent explanation as to why he was called is that the police hoped that his evidence, in juxtaposition with that of Robson, would mislead the jury into believing that Evelyn Foster had not driven to Belsay—indeed, had not even passed Knowesgate—but, alone in the car, had probably driven no farther than Wolf's Nick. Whether or not this explanation is correct, the presence—and the placing—of Harrison among the witnesses indicates that Philip Dodds, the coroner, either was a dunce at sums or had accepted without query a suggested list of witnesses, together with their statements, which the police submitted to him prior to the inquest.

Consider: Robson's 'about 7.22 . . . at Raylees' was no guess, but was based on his time-sheet for the journey, the farm being a 'time-check point' on the route. If the Hudson had continued at the same low speed—'no more than ten miles an hour'—it would not have reached Knowesgate, which is roughly six and a half miles from Raylees, until more than half an hour after Harrison's departure at 7.30. In order for the car to have been ahead of Harrison when he set off for Newcastle, it would have had suddenly to accelerate beyond Raylees and travel at an average speed of not less than 45 miles an hour—which in 1931 was a fast speed even in daylight and on a good surface, and which—at the present time, let alone in 1931—would be recklessly fast at night on a road made treacherous by an unusually heavy frost and patches of ice.

It is a mind-boggling proposition, but what the police appear to have wanted the jury to accept was that Evelyn Foster *could* have been seen by Harrison if after driving slowly for the first two miles from Otterburn, she had had a rush of blood to the head and driven like a maniac—or, as the Americans say, like an accident looking for somewhere to happen—for at least another six and a half miles. Thinking about it, the police case would have been immeasurably strengthened if Harrison *had* seen the Hudson coming back from Belsay, for this would have shewn that, only a short time before, the girl must have aberrated from her normally careful, even sedate, driving to such an extent as to signify a death-wish.

Though the Fosters were naturally anxious that the jury should return a verdict of murder, the three members of the family who gave evidence—Mr and Mrs Foster and their son Gordon—did not allow their anxiety to extend to a *determination* to obtain that verdict. They did not prevaricate; on several occasions they gave answers that were helpful to the police case when they might just as easily have either parried the questions or given concocted replies.

An instance of the almost naive truthfulness of the Fosters appears in Mr Smirk's examination of Joseph, who was the fourth witness of the day. Asked about Evelyn's return from Rochester and what she had told her mother concerning the man who wanted to be driven to Ponteland, Joseph agreed that, at the time, he had thought it strange that the man was not waiting at the garage. Joseph did not hesitate in giving this answer; nor did he point out that the thought was removed from his mind after only a moment or so by his wife's explaining that the man had gone to the Percy Arms in the hope of getting a free lift. Mr Smirk's next question depended on a non-sequitur: 'And whilst you would have expected the man to come to the garage, you did not see a man?' Since Joseph was not at the garage, but was sitting in the living-room of The Kennels, he could not possibly have seen who was or was not waiting there; he did not argue this point, however, but simply answered 'No'.

In case some charitably minded reader wishes to find an excuse for Mr Smirk's nonsensical question by assuming that the solicitor for the police was ignorant of Joseph Foster's whereabouts when Evelyn returned from Rochester, it should be said that Joseph's presence at The Kennels had been established during Mrs Foster's evidence and restated by Joseph himself, in answer to questions put to him by the coroner. Joseph added little to his wife's account of the episode; asked by Mr Dodds to explain why, if Evelyn was running her own business, she required him to 'make a quotation' for the fare to Ponteland, he said that 'she always looked for my advice. . . . I think it was just natural habit.'

He described Evelyn's car in these words:

It was her own car—a Hudson saloon Super-Six, with three gears forward and one reverse. A luggage chest was fastened to the back of the car; it was never locked. In this she kept a spare petrol can wrapped in a sack; it held two gallons; the can had a wire fastened to it, but I don't know if it was sealed. The can was a Pratt's can. I last saw it in the car about ten days before the tragedy, and it seemed intact. . . . The car was in perfect order.[2]

Joseph's assertion that the spare petrol was kept in a Pratt's can created yet another small mystery in the case. It is dangerous to discount evidence that is wholly dependent on a witness's memory simply because it is at odds with evidence that can be seen—in this instance, the *Shell* petrol can found at the rear of the car at Wolf's Nick and presented as an exhibit at the inquest. But it is surely inconceivable that the Shell can did not come from the Hudson's luggage box. If Joseph's memory was correct, then a possible explanation is that, some time after he saw the Pratt's can, Evelyn sold the spare petrol, can and all, to a stranded motorist, and replaced it with a can of Shell petrol when she returned to the garage.

The subject of the inquest was a woman hire-car driver, and eleven of the twenty-seven witnesses were connected in one way or another with cars or buses, or both. But Albert Beach, the last witness before the Monday luncheon adjournment, earned his living by driving a very different sort of vehicle: a steam-roller. It seems that Albert was almost inseparable from his steam-roller; if he had a permanent home, he did not sleep there (at least, not during the week) but stayed in a caravan—which, presumably, was towed from one lot of road-works to the next by the trusty steam-roller.

On the night of 6 January, the steam-roller and caravan were resting on a verge in Dere Street (the road that runs near Hexham from the south, then west of Otterburn, to meet the Otterburn–Jedburgh road at Elishaw); according to Albert's estimate, the resting-place was about a quarter of a mile from Elishaw Road Ends. He left the caravan at quarter to seven and started to walk to Otterburn for a drink at the Percy Arms; after he had walked about 300yd along the road towards Elishaw, 'a dark-blue, two-seater closed car' passed him, 'travelling very fast' in the direction of Hexham. He walked a few paces more along the road, then, turning right, took a short cut provided by a footpath across the fields in the V formed by the junction of Dere Street and the Otterburn-Jedburgh road. 'Only about five minutes—perhaps less' after seeing the first car, he saw another, ahead of him across the fields, travelling from Elishaw towards Otterburn.

Now, Albert Beach's evidence reads for all the world as if it were a first-term test for aspiring advocates: the sort of test that is headed by the instruction, 'Read the following in thirty seconds and suggest questions that might be put to the witness.' The answers—or replies—to the questions that spring to mind could well have assisted the jury in evaluating the story: in weighing whether or not the first car Albert Beach saw could have been the one driven by the 'mystery woman' and whether or not the second could have been Evelyn Foster's Hudson. It is not at all surprising that Mr Smirk did not ask any of these questions, for the answers were far more likely to have harmed the police case than to have assisted it; it *is* surprising that the coroner allowed Albert Beach to leave the witness stand with his evidence unrefined: but what is more surprising is that no questions were put by Mr Bates—who, in case the reader has forgotten his presence at the proceedings, was supposed to be acting on behalf of the Foster family. Whatever Mr Bates's characteristics, loquacity was not one of them; he is reported as having asked three questions during the first day of the inquest, and exceeded this number only slightly during the second and third days.

An elementary rule of advocacy is that one should never ask a question unless one already knows the answer, but Mr Bates had everything to gain and nothing to lose by breaking this rule in an attempt to clarify the evidence of Albert Beach.

The first question that Mr Bates should have asked was whether Beach was quite sure that the car going towards Hexham was a two-seater—or rather, a car in which only two people could travel—for the car Evelyn Foster claimed to have seen at Elishaw must have been capable of holding three, perhaps four, people: the woman driver and one or two male passengers in addition to the man who alighted. If Beach's answer had been an unequivocal yes, then it would have been worth querying his recollection of details by asking how he was able to distinguish dark-blue from black at night on an unlit road. He may, of course, have been carrying a torch; even so, it would have needed to be a very strong one—and he would still have had to be blessed with exceptional eyesight—for him to tell the two colours apart.

Beach should also have been asked if he noticed whether the second car was travelling at all faster when it went out of sight than when he first saw it. An affirmative answer could have been taken as an indication that the car was the Hudson, gathering speed after being stationary at Elishaw.

Lastly, Beach should have been questioned regarding his estimate of the time that elapsed between his seeing the two cars: 'about five minutes—perhaps less'. What margin of error was signified by 'perhaps less'? If only a minute or so, as the words suggest, then it would seem unlikely that *both* the cars were associated with Evelyn's claimed meeting with the man at Elishaw: nothing of what she told her mother gives the impression that she left the Hudson to talk to the man—or that, when the man had entered the car, they exchanged more than a few words before she continued her journey to Otterburn. But how reliable was Beach's perception of lapse of time? Though academic experiments show that the vast majority of people have inaccurate 'mental clocks' and that the general tendency is to over-estimate lapse of time, it would be false to argue from such general findings that a particular steam-roller driver was a poor judge of time. Beach's estimate should, of course, have been tested by the police soon after he made his statement; but as this was not done, Mr Bates ought to have asked the coroner's permission for the witness temporarily to leave the stand and be driven to the place in Dere Street where he was passed by the car, from there to retrace his steps to the approximate position from which he saw the second car, while an observer timed him.

In the absence of answers to the questions mentioned above, all one can say about Albert Beach's evidence is that if the two cars he saw were unconnected with the case, then it is a rather strange coincidence that, with the roads near Otterburn almost deserted of traffic, the cars reached Elishaw and diverged at a time that accorded with Evelyn Foster's account.

The next three witnesses all had something to say about Evelyn's return to the garage from Rochester.

George Maughan, the assistant at the village Co-op, said that 'at about 6.30' he and his wife were walking northwards along the road 'near' the garage when he saw a car, which he took to be Evelyn's, drive up to the door: 'I saw no one in the car but the lady driving.' He added that he 'saw the car approaching the garage some time before,' but the ambiguity of this remark does not seem to have been cleared up: either he meant that he saw the car's headlights on the road outside the village some time before it pulled up at the garage, or that the car approached the garage some time before he and his wife arrived there. Maughan remembered that between his house (which was close to the church) and the garage, he met two men walking in the opposite direction to himself and his wife (that is, in the direction of the Percy Arms): 'I recognised one as the schoolmaster, but not the other.'

Maughan was the first witness to whom Mr Bates addressed a question: 'Considering that it was night, would you have been able to see anyone in the back of the car?' Maughan said 'No,' and Mr Bates, who must have been quivering with delight at the success of his debut, resumed his seat.

Mr Smirk asked: 'Am I correct in thinking that the man you met on the way to the garage but did not recognise at first was a man named John Thompson?' 'Yes,' said Maughan, who then left the witness stand and was replaced by Thompson, a young farm labourer.

Thompson was not sure what time it was when he passed the garage, but he remembered seeing a car there: 'I took it to be Evelyn's and heard a voice which I thought was hers. I did not see who she was talking to, only that he was wearing a pair of leggings. I believe that another man I saw near the car was Mr Maughan.'

The last of this trio of witnesses was Robert Luke, one of the Foster bus drivers, who said that he saw Mr and Mrs Maughan pass the garage at about seven o'clock; he noticed the Hudson parked in the forecourt, but did not see anyone sitting in the car.

The evidence of Maughan and Thompson will be considered in detail in the next chapter. For the present, the only comment that needs to be made concerns the half-hour difference between the time at which Maughan said he saw the Hudson arriving at the garage— 'about 6.30'—and the time at which Luke said he saw the Maughans passing by. Clearly, Luke's estimate was pretty accurate (he was able to reckon the time in relation to his return to the garage at the end of a scheduled bus journey). But it is difficult to know what to make of Maughan's estimate, which put the time of Evelyn Foster's return to the garage back to the time at which she set off for Rochester with the three passengers who had alighted from Cecil Johnstone's bus; were it not for Luke's evidence, one might almost wonder whether Maughan had some peculiar disease of the eye which caused certain receding objects to appear to be coming towards him.

A question of time was also raised by the evidence of William Kirsopp-Reid, the Otterburn farmer whose car Evelyn had told her mother she had seen at Belsay shortly before the man ordered her to turn back (see page 43).

Kirsopp-Reid told the coroner: 'On the evening of the tragedy I was driving home from Newcastle via Belsay. About 200 yards north of Belsay, about 7.20, I met a car at Ferney Chesters. I also met a saloon car which might have been Miss Foster's Hudson, but I cannot say for certain.'

In examining this witness, Mr Smirk seemed to achieve his greatest success of the day. After pointing out that if John Robson, the bus driver, saw the Hudson at Raylees, two miles from Otterburn, at 7.22, Kirsopp-Reid could not possibly have seen the same car at Ferney Chesters, more than ten miles away, at 7.20, the solicitor for the police tidied things up with two questions:

'Are you prepared to say that the time you have given is accurate within certain limits?'

'Yes,' the farmer replied.

'A maximum of five minutes' accuracy?'

Again, 'Yes'.

But there was more to Mr Smirk's success than apparently establishing that Evelyn could not have seen—or been seen by—the farmer at Belsay. Needing a possible explanation as to how she could have known of Kirsopp-Reid's presence on the road if she did not see him, Mr Smirk asked:

'Do you happen to know if Miss Foster, or anyone closely associated with her, knew that you were going to Newcastle that day?'

'Gordon, probably.'

'The dead girl's brother?'

'That's right.'

Mr Smirk's double-triumph was spectacular—but only in the sense of being showy. If Mr Bates had been a competent adversary—if, indeed, he had simply done a little homework before the inquest—the two points could have been negated, or at least undermined.

Let us look at the second point first. When Gordon Foster gave evidence, Mr Bates did not ask him whether he knew in advance of Kirsopp-Reid's trip to Newcastle—and, if he did, whether he mentioned it to his sister. Had Mr Bates been less reticent during the proceedings, the absence of the question might indicate that Gordon did know and had told his sister; but Mr Bates failed to ask so many questions of greater importance that one cannot even hazard a guess as to whether the omission of this one was deliberate or not.

But suppose Evelyn did know that Kirsopp-Reid was going to Newcastle that day, this still does not explain how she knew that he would be returning within a fairly narrow period during the evening. More important—because her reference to seeing him was to show that she had driven as far as Belsay—prior knowledge of Kirsopp-Reid's trip would not have given her a reliable indication of the time when he would be driving through Belsay.[3]

If the police theory was correct (that Evelyn did not drive far past Wolf's Nick but, knowing that Kirsopp-Reid was returning home about that time, determined to pretend that she had seen him at Belsay), then it is necessary to accept that she must have reversed into a side-road so as to see Kirsopp-Reid's car go by without being seen by him—first, to be sure that he was past Wolf's Nick before she set fire to the Hudson, second, to be sure that he was really on the road at a time that would support her story of seeing him at Belsay.

This leads us back to the first point. If Kirsopp-Reid's estimate of the time when he passed through Belsay was accurate, then Evelyn, waiting in a side-road near Wolf's Nick, saw his car pass at a much earlier time than she expected—a time that she must have realised was far too early for him to have been at Belsay when she could have been there. The only way of keeping the police theory alive is to assume that Evelyn's mind was confused when she was questioned by her mother, and she blurted out that she had seen Kirsopp-Reid at Belsay, completely forgetting that before starting her fire-raising activities she had realised that this story was untenable.

Just how reliable was Kirsopp-Reid's estimate? As we know, he said that he was at Belsay at about 7.20, and he replied 'Yes' to Mr Smirk's 'A maximum of five minutes' accuracy?' But would he have given five minutes as the margin of error if the question had not been a leading one? Would he have changed his mind if Mr Bates had started a sort of forensic auction by asking if he was prepared to give any advance on five minutes?

The time of 7.20 appears to have been based on either the time of his departure from Newcastle or the time of his arrival at his farm in Otterburn; whichever it was, in all probability the 'basis time' was assumed rather than known, since if he had consulted a watch or clock at the start of his journey, during it, or as soon as he got home, he would surely have mentioned this to the police—and if the remembered *actual* time had been corroborative of his being at Belsay at 7.20, Mr Smirk would have brought it out during the questioning. The likelihood, then, is that the 'Belsay time' was an estimate based on an estimate.

Was Kirsopp-Reid any better at judging time than distance? In his evidence to the coroner, he said: 'About 200yd north of Belsay, about 7.20, I met a car at Ferney Chesters.' Perhaps because the words 'Belsay, about 7.20' deflected everyone's minds from the rest of the sentence, the bit about Ferney Chesters was not queried. If it had been, no doubt a map would have been produced—and the hamlet of Ferney Chesters would have been seen to be a good deal farther from Belsay than 200yd: nearly four miles, in fact.

The magnitude of the error extends the implications. The excessive under-estimate shows that Kirsopp-Reid was a hopeless judge of distance—but more than that, it must cast doubt on his powers of perception in general.

The evidence of the farmer, Kirsopp-Reid, was followed by that of a shepherd, Sidney Henderson, who lived in a cottage on Harwood Head, a discreet peak of the Ottercops, about two miles north of Wolf's Nick. He said that at about quarter to nine on the night of 6 January he saw a fire 'burning brightly' at Wolf's Nick, but being too far away to make out what fuelled the flames, assumed that 'it was a fire made by campers'. Henderson's evidence was left like this. Neither the coroner nor either of the solicitors asked him the one question that was at all important: Had he looked across at Wolf's Nick at any time shortly before about quarter to nine? If the answer had been yes—and if the shepherd had been able to say roughly how long before—it would have given an indication of the period of time in which the fire started. As it was, Henderson was treated simply as a formal witness to the fact that the car was alight at a time that fitted both Evelyn Foster's statement and the police theory.

The last witnesses of the day were Cecil Johnstone, Thomas Rutherford and Thomas Vasey; nothing of what they said amplifies or contradicts what the reader already knows about the events in the three hours or so following the discovery of Evelyn Foster at Wolf's Nick.

Right to the end, Mr Smirk was trying to obscure facts that did not assist the police theory: to confuse the jury into believing what he knew to be untrue. Vasey told the coroner that when he went to Wolf's Nick with Johnstone and the police at 1 am on 7 January, he 'decided then that the car was either in gear, or the gear box had melted'. Mr Smirk's first question to the mechanic was 'Did you say that the car was in gear?' 'I said I thought it was or that the gear box was wrong,' Vasey replied. Mr Smirk then asked, apparently casually: 'If the gear box was not melted, you say the car was not in gear?' Hearing the question he expected rather than the one that was asked, Vasey replied 'Yes,' and the police solicitor at once switched to a different subject. Fortunately, Mr Bates noticed—or had it pointed out to him—that the witness had been fooled into saying 'Yes' instead of 'No'; even more fortunately, considering his reticence, he decided that he had better ask Vasey what gear the Hudson was in, and received the reply: 'I did not know the gear positions then, but do now, and it was in low gear.'

That night, at The Kennels, Gordon and Joseph Foster had an argument. Gordon contended that the family would be better off with no legal representative rather than to allow Mr Bates to continue. He believed that the solicitor was not simply useless to the cause of proving that Evelyn had been murdered but positively harmful to it, since the jury would infer that if a man employed to ask questions remained silent, it was because there were no questions to ask.

Joseph agreed with his son's criticisms, but refused to countenance the idea of replacing Mr Bates, who had acted as the firm's legal adviser for some years, his main tasks relating to the licensing of the bus services. Joseph pointed out that it would be impossible to 'sack Bates quietly': the press would make headlines from this action, and it would cause untold damage to the solicitor's practice—indeed, might even ruin him.[4]

In the end, it was agreed that, the following morning, before the inquest resumed, Joseph should take Mr Bates aside and tell him to 'buck his ideas up'.

Presuming that this admonition was given, Mr Bates must have been either unwilling or unable to take it to heart.

*Tuesday, 3 February*

The proceedings re-opened with the evidence of a road mender called John Kennedy, who said that he spent the early evening of 6 January at Kirkwhelpington, the village set back from the Otterburn–Newcastle road about four miles south-east of Wolf's Nick. Leaving Kirkwhelpington at eight o'clock, he set off on the mile-and-a-half walk to his cottage at Knowesgate, the nearest hamlet to Wolf's Nick:

> As I was returning home—this would be about ten past eight—two cars passed me going south. Then a saloon car overtook me at a high speed, travelling north in the direction of Otterburn. I noticed that a man was driving, but saw no one else in the car; I am unable to say whether the driver wore a bowler hat or any head covering. I can only remember the numbers 1 and 3 on the number plate.

Had the road mender seen Evelyn Foster's Hudson—TN 8135—returning from Belsay after the passenger had taken control? Mr Smirk's determination to disabuse the jury of this notion was manifested by a tone of ostentatiously suppressed anger; every inflection indicated that he considered Kennedy a liar. The police had provided him with two lines of attack, and he chose to use the one that seemed strongest first:

'Do you know a Mr William Herdman?'

'Yes.'

'And do you know that Mr Herdman drives a car with the registration number BR 6123?'

'Yes,' Kennedy said—then, before Mr Smirk quite realised what was happening, proceeded to make further discussion of Herdman's car irrelevant: 'I can definitely say that it was not his car that I saw—and I don't think he would drive at such a furious pace. In any case, the 1 and 3 were together on the car that overtook me.'

Mr Smirk abruptly switched to an attack on Kennedy's credit as a witness:

'Were you at the scene of the fire on the following day, the Wednesday?'

'Yes, I was.'

'Did you ever mention to the police that you had seen a car the previous night?'

'I am not sure.'

'I suggest to you that you never mentioned to the police that you had seen a car until the police approached you about ten days later.'

'I would not like to be definite about that point.'

'Why not? You are definite upon other points.'

'I am rather under the impression that I mentioned to the constable on duty next morning that I had seen a car.'

'I suggest you never mentioned it.'

'I am hazy about it.'

'I suggest you never mentioned that you had seen a car until you were approached ten days later.'

'It's possible.'

Two questions arise from this exchange. Firstly, was Kennedy's professed uncertainty actually equivocation? The answer appears to be yes. Secondly, does the assumption that he did not give information to the police at Wolf's Nick on the Wednesday—and the knowledge that he did not make an official statement until he was approached ten days later—give cause for suspecting the reliability of his evidence about the car? The answer appears to be no. Mr Smirk used an old forensic trick of making a relatively unimportant point seem vital, and it may be that Kennedy, knowing that his main evidence was true, fell into the trap of *trying* to protect it; in many trial transcripts there are instances of witnesses falling into the same trap.

One of Kennedy's answers strongly suggests that if he had kept his head and admitted that he had not given information to the police on the Wednesday, he could also have explained *why* he had not done so. He said: 'I am rather under the impression that I mentioned to the constable on duty next morning that I had seen a car.' This answer, with its reference to 'the constable on duty', seems to indicate that Kennedy was at Wolf's Nick very early on the Wednesday morning: between seven o'clock, the time at which Robert Pringle saw the constable arriving to guard the scene of the crime, and eight, when the first contingent of 'investigating policemen' turned up. Even if the constable was more talkative to Kennedy than to Pringle, whom he simply told to 'move along', it is extremely unlikely that he had been briefed about the night's events and could have given Kennedy any details that might have prompted the road mender to mention the car that had passed him near Kirkwhelpington. Kennedy, of course, might have seen a copy of the *North Mail*, the only morning newspaper to carry an account of the case—but a reading of this would have led him to believe that his sighting of a car at ten minutes past eight the previous night had no bearing on the case, for the account wrongly stated that the incident at Wolf's Nick occurred at about seven.

During the days that followed, it must have become clear to Kennedy that his information could be of importance, yet he still did not pass it on to the police; presumably, if they had not approached him, he would never have made a statement. According to Mr Smirk's way of thinking, the evidence of so reluctant a witness could not be relied upon. But what possible reason could Kennedy have had for inventing the story about the car? The very fact that he did not volunteer the information rules out the idea that he was an inventive publicity-seeker, and the idea that someone acting for the Fosters, with or without their knowledge, persuaded him or paid him to commit perjury can be eliminated on the same ground. What other possible reason is left?

Kennedy was followed on the witness stand by William Herdman, the farmer whose car's registration number included the digits 1 and 3. Kennedy had said that he did not think Herdman would drive at such a furious pace as did the driver of the car he saw, and this point seems to have been borne out by Herdman himself, who said that he left Kirkwhelpington at ten minutes past eight and reached his home, four and a half miles away, at 8.30; his average speed, then, was between 13–14 miles an hour. In answer to a question from the coroner, Herdman said that he did not see any vehicles as he was driving northwards along the Newcastle–Otterburn road. What he was *not* asked was whether he remembered overtaking Kennedy. This omission is an astonishing one, for the sole purpose of calling Herdman as a witness was to show that the car Kennedy saw might have been his. It seems hardly likely that Herdman, driving at such a slow speed, could not have noticed Kennedy (with whom he was on speaking terms); indeed, Herdman is remembered as 'a friendly sort of chap,' and the probability is that if he *had* seen Kennedy, he would have offered him a lift as far as Knowesgate.

The next witness to be called was Walter Smith Beattie: but why he was called at all is something of a mystery. Beattie, who was a car dealer in Hawick, across the border, stated that on 6 January he collected a Morris Cowley car at Darlington and in the evening returned to Hawick by way of the Newcastle–Otterburn road. He reckoned that he passed Wolf's Nick between half-past nine and ten (it will be remembered that Cecil Johnstone's bus reached there at the latter time). Seeing the burning car, he 'slowed down by using the foot-brake'—then, deciding that 'it was an ordinary burn-out and that the car had been abandoned,' he drove on.

If Beattie had seen anyone moving about near the car, his evidence would have been relevant—but no, 'it was clear moonlight,' he told the coroner, 'and not a soul did I see.'

If the Morris's brake had squealed when Beattie pulled up, this might have explained Evelyn Foster's statement (according to Constable Fegusson) that while she was lying on the ground she heard a car pull up and someone whistle. But Beattie told the coroner, 'I do not think the brake squealed when applied'—and later, in answer to a question from a member of the jury, said that he was *certain* that the brake made no sound. Since there was no way of proving that Beattie was the only driver who pulled up at Wolf's Nick between the time the fire started and the arrival of the bus, his negative evidence gave no support to the conclusion reached by the police that the sound which Evelyn Foster claimed to have heard was not caused by a brake—nor, for that matter, by a person unconnected with the crime whistling in the hope of attracting the attention of anyone in the vicinity. The police, having decided—rather than proved—that Beattie was the only 'innocent traveller' who had stopped at Wolf's Nick, left themselves with two ways of explaining Evelyn Foster's reference to the whistle: either the bowler-hatted man had an accomplice (which, considering the nature and circumstances of the crime, seemed almost impossibly unlikely) or Evelyn Foster did not hear a whistle but said that she did as one lie among many. *Reductio ad absurdum.*

Following Beattie, Gordon Foster gave evidence that was chiefly concerned with his two conversations with Evelyn on the night of 6 January, the first at about half-past six, before she drove to Rochester, and the second when she was brought home in the bus. There is nothing in his evidence that the reader does not already know.

The same applies to the evidence of the next two witnesses. First, Constable Andrew Fergusson, who described his actions and observations following the telephone call from Joseph Foster at quarter to eleven; read aloud his 194-word, potted version of Evelyn Foster's statement; and said that, though he had made 'careful investigations of farms and outbuildings in the neighbourhood', he had found no one answering Evelyn's description of her assailant, and that 'numerous telephone calls and inquiries' had failed to trace anyone who had seen such a person. Second, Constable Henry Proud, whose testimony related to the first police visit to Wolf's Nick, at one o'clock on the Wednesday morning.

A third constable, William Turnbull, stated that he guarded Wolf's Nick on the Wednesday *night*. This testimony was so audaciously irrelevant that a good many people who attended the inquest or read newspaper reports of the proceedings must have been misled into thinking that the scene of the crime was guarded at a time that really mattered.

The fourth of a quartet of police witnesses was Inspector Edward Russell, whose evidence to the coroner was mainly of a formal nature: a recitation of measurements he had taken at Wolf's Nick and a description of various exhibits found in and around the car. The inspector pointed out that 'there was no sign of burning of the heather between the main road and the car,' and concluded from this that the car had 'taken fire where it stood'.

This conclusion, of course, was in opposition to Evelyn Foster's implicit statement that the fire was started while the car was parked on the road. Seeking to reinforce the police theory that the girl drove the car on to the moors and *then* set fire to it, using the can of petrol from the luggage box, Mr Smirk asked the inspector to look at the neck of the can:[5]

Is it scorched or not inside?—No.

On the outside?—Slightly.

The screw-cap of the tin was not scorched in the slightest? —No.

The threads of the neck and the threads of the cap are intact and undamaged?—Yes.

Those two exhibits, the neck and the cap, were lying apart from each other at the rear of the car?—Yes.

If the cap had been screwed on the neck, could it, having regard to its condition, have become separated without being unscrewed?—No.

Their condition—that is, one scorched by fire and the other not scorched— indicates that they must have been unscrewed before the fire?—Yes.

Mr Smirk then asked two questions to remind the jury that there was no sign of burning in the car tracks on the moors and, with a what-more-needs-to-be-said? expression on his face, sat down.

In fact, quite a lot more needs to be said about this evidence. The first thing is that the absence of burn marks in the car tracks cannot be taken as an indication that the car was not on fire when it left the road. The fire started inside the car, at the back, and it is probable—not just possible—that the flames would not have escaped outside the car *and underneath it* during the journey of 198ft; even at the slowest possible forward speed—less than walking pace—the car would have taken under a minute to cover this distance.

But let us, just for a moment, assume that this part of the police theory was correct: that the fire was not started until the car had come to a halt on the moor. Whether the fire-raiser was Evelyn Foster or her passenger, the sequence of activities must have been as follows: (1) the petrol can was taken from the luggage box and the cap unscrewed; (2) the petrol was poured over the back seats of the car; (3) the can was either replaced in the luggage box or put on top of it (the can was found among the debris of the box and the carrier platform) and the cap dropped or thrown on the ground a foot or so from the rear of the car; (4) the petrol was ignited. (If the fire-raiser was the passenger, then activities 3 and 4 could have been transposed.) The fact that the can was replaced in the luggage box, or put on top of it, rather than being simply dropped on the ground, suggests, at first sight, that the fire-raiser either was obsessionally tidy or hoped that putting the can back where it belonged would cast doubts in the investigators' minds as to whether its contents had been used to start the fire. But both explanations are ruled out by the finding of the screw-cap away from the can.

Actually, discussion as to why the fire-raiser bothered to put the empty petrol can in or on the luggage box is pointless—because it is plain from answers given by Inspector Russell to Mr Smirk that *the place where the police found the can was not the place where it was left at the time of the crime.* Clearly, someone visited Wolf's Nick when the fire was almost out, picked up the can from wherever it was lying, and dropped it on the ground at the rear of the car, among the charred remains of the luggage box and its carrier platform.

The reason for saying this is simple. Russell stated that the neck of the can was not scorched at all on the inside, and was only slightly scorched on the outside. Unlike so much of the evidence, the inspector's answers can be relied upon, for he had the exhibit in front of him—he said what he saw, not what he remembered. Amazingly, it did not occur to the police—nor to anyone else, for that matter—that if the open can had been in or on the luggage box during the fire, then the outside of the neck would have been far more than 'slightly' scorched, and the inside would not have remained unscathed. (The slight scorching of the outside of the neck indicates that when the can was dropped in the debris, the neck came in contact with embers of the luggage box. The vapours of the vestiges of petrol in the can would almost certainly have escaped, and if they had caught light, would have done so some measurable distance from the neck.)

The reader will remember that, according to Cecil Johnstone, when he and Tommy Rutherford were at Wolf's Nick at ten o'clock, both the nearside doors of the Hudson were closed; but when Johnstone returned with the police three hours later, the front nearside door was open. One wonders whether the person who moved the petrol can also opened the door. Or was there more than one inquisitive visitor? Presumably, if anyone had made a statement to the police that they visited the scene of the crime before 10 pm, they would have been called as a witness at the inquest in preference to Walter Beattie—but did no one come forward to say that they were at Wolf's Nick between 10 pm and 1 am? Though there were few travellers on the road that night, it is hard to believe that for a period of three hours no one apart from the person who moved the petrol can considered a burning or burnt-out car (still smoking at 1 am) of sufficient interest to warrant inspection.

The day's proceedings ended with further evidence from witnesses who had appeared earlier.

Joseph Foster was recalled to give details of his daughter's finances and to produce insurance policies covering the Hudson. He said that, as Evelyn's account book had been destroyed in the fire, he could give no idea of her earnings. He had, however, obtained a statement of her account at Lloyd's Bank, Bellingham, and a note of her credit in the Post Office Savings Bank; the two amounts totalled £489 10s od.

Joseph explained that the Hudson was insured under two 'floating' policies which covered all vehicles owned by his firm ('We . . . get a cheaper rate by insuring in my name, but the insurance people understood that the car was Evelyn's.') One policy insured vehicles while they were in the garage; the other, as interpreted by the coroner, insured 'any car up to 30 hp belonging to [the] company against fire, theft or accident on the road, up to £700 as a maximum, but the amount payable [was] to be arranged according to current values'.

(One of the theories seeking to explain what happened at Wolf's Nick was—and is—that Evelyn was in need of money and therefore decided to defraud the insurance company by destroying her car and putting the blame on a mythical passenger; in setting fire to the car, she accidentally caused her own death. The theory, though severely wounded by the evidence that Evelyn had nearly £500 in the two banks, was kept alive by the belief that the current value of the Hudson was in the region of £300. 'She may have had £500,' the proponents of the theory argued, 'but suppose she desperately needed, say, £800 for a reason she could not disclose to her family or to a friend?' There are two facts which would seem to destroy the theory. The first is that Evelyn Foster was far better off than her bank balances suggested: her will was probated at £1,442 gross. The second is that the General Accident Assurance Co's assessment of the current value of the Hudson was a mere £45.)

John Kennedy was also recalled—by, of all people, the uninquisitive Mr Bates. Someone must have pointed out to the solicitor supposedly representing the Fosters that he had neglected to ask the road mender a rather vital question. Now he was allowed to remedy the omission. Referring to the driver of the car that had passed Kennedy near Kirkwhelpington, he asked: 'Did you observe how he was sitting?'

'He seemed to be sitting more sideways than straight on at his wheel,' Kennedy replied.

For two days, Mr Bates had not asked enough questions; now he asked one too many—a garbled one at that. 'Was there anything which broke your line of vision? I suggest that there might have been luggage or a person in the car.'

Kennedy's reply was 'I couldn't say,' and when Mr Smirk rose to examine, he made sure that the reply was implanted in the jurymen's minds by putting three versions of Mr Bates's question to the witness.

Then followed perhaps the most disgraceful incident at the inquest. Not receiving the answers he wanted to two further questions, Mr

Smirk asked another question after each 'wrong' answer; each of the supplementary questions was intended to confuse the witness and was framed around *invented* evidence.

The first legitimate question was 'Do you say that the car you saw was a dark car?', to which Kennedy replied: 'It appeared to be dark in the moonlight.'

Though Mr Smirk was well aware that the Hudson was painted black, he then asked: 'Do you realise that the late Miss Foster's car was a light-coloured car?' 'No,' the witness said.

The second legitimate question, 'Was the car being driven fast?', was answered with a 'yes'.

Knowing quite well that Evelyn Foster had said nothing regarding the speed at which the man drove the Hudson back from Belsay, Mr Smirk asked: 'Do you realise that it has been put in evidence that the late Miss Foster said that the man she referred to drove slowly?' 'No,' Kennedy replied.

Neither of the tricks worked—but in trying to confuse Kennedy, Mr Smirk could well have misled some member or members of the jury into believing that what he said in the supplementary questions was true. Even if the coroner did not consider Mr Smirk's tactics sufficiently shoddy to warrant a rebuke, he should have at least pointed out to the jury that the questions were founded on fiction. But Mr Dodds said nothing. And, needless to say, there was no objection by Mr Bates.

When the inquest was adjourned late on Tuesday afternoon, only three witnesses remained to be called. The public was informed by the press that two of these witnesses—Professor Stuart McDonald, the pathologist, and William Jennings, the motor engineer—were 'confidently expected to unfold dramatic and unexpected facts'. But this evidence would have to wait a day because on Wednesday Mr Dodds's presence was required at the Whitley Bay Police Court, where he was clerk to the magistrates.

### Thursday, 5 February
Throughout the country, and especially in Northumberland, cars of one sort or another must have formed the day's main topic of conversation. The front pages of the morning papers carried accounts of how,

on the previous day, at Daytona Beach, Florida, Captain Malcolm Campbell had driven his car, 'Blue Bird', to a world land-speed record of 246·154mph. The evening papers would devote many columns to reports of the last day of the inquest on the death of Evelyn Foster, a substantial part of which was taken up by evidence concerning the Hudson hire-car. And as part of the 'human interest' reporting of the inquest, the evening papers would describe how the police car taking Captain Fullarton James's party to Otterburn skidded and overturned on an icy stretch of road a mile or so past Wolf's Nick. Shaken but unharmed, the Chief Constable and his men clambered out through a window, managed to rock the car back on to its wheels, and drove on at a careful speed.

Though the proceedings had begun by the time they arrived at the War Memorial Hall, they did not miss anything of importance. The first witness, Dr Duncan McEachran, gave wholly unsurprising evidence as to his observation of the burns on the body of the dying girl and his recollection of snatches of what she said during the interview conducted by Mrs Foster. The most important point made by the doctor was in answer to a question from a member of the jury. As McEachran was about to leave the stand, the juryman asked if Evelyn had actually said that she was knocked unconscious by the man, and the doctor replied: 'No; what she did say was that she became unconscious after being knocked into the back of the car.'

When reporters use the phrase, 'a stir in court', it usually means no more than that they themselves stirred. But the words were appropriate to the spectators' reaction to the calling of Professor Stuart McDonald, for during the past couple of weeks there had been greater speculation, more rumour, about the pathologist's findings than about the rest of the evidence put together.

The professor began his evidence by reading from a report. This dealt, first of all, with the burns on the body of Evelyn Foster, as he had observed them at the post-mortem examination on 8 January:

> The distribution of the burns and their severity in certain places suggested that certain portions of the clothing had contained some inflammable substance.

Confirmation of this opinion was provided by a chemical examination of pieces of clothing found at Wolf's Nick:

The oil present on the exhibits is almost entirely human fat. At the same time, a petroleum oil observed in two exhibits, considered in conjunction with the fat that had distilled, affords clear evidence of the presence of a trace of a light petroleum distillate.

The burning had started in front of the body and was most severe on the upper and inner aspects of the thighs, and, generally speaking, diminished in an upward and downward direction, though both hands and the face were severely burnt. The left foot and ankle were practically free from evidence of burning, but the right ankle and the top of the right foot showed superficial burning and blistering. There was evidence of burning as high as the breast; above the breast there were definitely localised areas, the largest being about the size of a half-crown piece.[6]

The distribution of the burned area on the lower portion of the buttocks and the absence of burning on the upper portion of the buttocks suggested that the deceased had been sitting during some period of the burning. Further, the absence of burning on the upper part of the chest, below the chin, together with the burning of the face, might be accounted for by a bending forward of the head.

The second part of the report read as follows:

There were no external marks suggesting injuries other than from burns on any part of the body; but over the burnt areas, superficial injuries or scratches could not possibly have been recognised. The features of the face were swollen and obscured by the burns, and there appeared to be a blueish discoloration about the roof of the nose and the upper part of the eyelids.

The third part of the report was the briefest:

I examined the deceased for evidence of sexual interference but came to the conclusion that she was virgo intacta; there was no evidence of violation.

The report ended with the results of tests carried out on articles found at Wolf's Nick.

The makeshift courtroom was absolutely silent as McDonald carefully folded the sheets of paper, put them in his inside breast pocket, and waited for the coroner's questions.

During the first two days of the inquest, Mr Dodds had given the impression that he disbelieved Evelyn Foster's statement but was doing his best to appear impartial. Now, however, the insubstantial mask of neutrality fell away as he pressed the pathologist to give answers that supported what he, Mr Dodds, believed to be the truth of the matter:

So far as any blows or smacking of the face is concerned, as suggested by the deceased, there was no trace of any bruising from that cause?—I could not find any trace of that.

If it had been at all severe, you could have found it?—Any severe injury, certainly, I think would have left a mark.

Any blow or injury which would have been strong enough to have stunned her?—I certainly would have expected to find something. Of course, I pointed out in my report that anything superficial could not possibly be detected. I found no evidence of any deep bruising.

If a girl was knocked out or stunned by a blow or other rough usage, you would probably find some trace?—I think one would reasonably have expected it.

In no shape or form was there any evidence of injury or interference?—No.

There was absolutely no sign of outrage?—None whatever.

Professor, the story of the girl was that at the time she was in the car with this man at Wolf's Nick, he hit her and threw her over the car seat, and then she said he threw something over her and she remembered nothing more until she was wakened by bumping. Could you tell by her burns if the girl could have been sitting or lying in the back seat?—It is possible, but I have not heard exactly what her story was.

Incidentally, would there be any trace of nipping?—The left arm was not burnt, and had there been any severe injury, one would have had a good chance of seeing it. There was no indication of it.

Could these burns have been caused by her in the back of the car?—If she were lying in the back of the car on the seat with her head forward like *this* [*the witness rested his chin on his chest*], I could conceive of such injuries as I found being produced in that way.

On the other hand, Professor, if no burning took place in the way she alleged in the back of the car, and assuming the car was standing where she put it, and the door was open, and she threw some petrol into the back of the car and then set fire to it, with her left leg probably on the running board, could the flames have come back that way?—I think that is possible, yes.

Quite possible?—Of course, I cannot quite understand, if that were the explanation, why there should have been localisation of the burns.

Referring to the point of localisation, it would signify to you that there had been something poured over that portion?—That is what is suggested.

Assuming she herself had upset some petrol over the lower part of her clothing and then had ignited the car, which had already been soaked with petrol, that would have been a possible cause?—Yes.

Is it not a possible solution, assuming she put the petrol on?—Yes.

And if she had taken the petrol tin and poured petrol over herself in that way, is it possible that she might have got those extra splashes on the top above the breast?—That is possible.

Mr Smirk decided that, in view of the sterling efforts of the coroner, he need only ask three questions:

It has been stated that the deceased was outraged. You say she was not?—That is so.

And she was absolutely a virgin?—The appearances I found were in every respect compatible with virginity.

The mother stated that the girl told her that the man began knocking her about and nipping her arm. Was there any evidence of that?—I found no such evidence.


Now the sedentary Mr Bates rose to his feet. There were any number of obvious questions that he could—and should—have put to Professor McDonald; he asked none of them. Looking at the questions that he did ask, one feels that it was as well for the Fosters that he asked so few others during the proceedings.

The first question was wholly inappropriate to the witness: 'Professor, we know that the petrol tin was found on the luggage carrier of the car. If Miss Foster had poured petrol over the car and on to her clothing, and then put the tin back in the luggage carrier, would not the petrol on her clothing have evaporated before she returned to the car?'

'I do not think so,' said McDonald, who knew nothing whatsoever about the speed of evaporation of petrol.[7]

Mr Bates's next three questions raised a most unlikely proposition: that though there would have been virtually no chance of Evelyn Foster's being heard if she had cried out after the car stopped at the roadside at Wolf's Nick, her assailant might have taken the trouble to gag her. Mr Bates's idea was that the scarf found at the scene could have been used for this purpose. Professor McDonald agreed that this was a possibility, but pointed out that there was no scintilla of evidence to support it.

Without pause, Mr Bates asked his final question—which, in juxtaposition with the three earlier ones, could well have made the jury wonder whether the scarf explained the absence of burns on Evelyn Foster's neck: 'And I take it that there were no marks on the neck of the girl to show that there had been any pressure there?' The reply was in the negative.

After answering a couple of questions from members of the jury, Professor McDonald left the stand.

What did his evidence amount to? What conclusions can be drawn from it? Let us look at each of the three main subject areas of his report:

## 1 The burns

The professor's evidence tallied with that part of Evelyn Foster's statement in which she said that she was sitting or lying unconscious on the back seat of the car when the fire started. His observation of the *absence* of burns on certain parts of the body was as important as his observation of the *presence* of burns on others: absent on the upper portion of the buttocks—present on the lower; absent on the neck and below the chin (the latter surface would not have been protected by the scarf, if she was wearing it)—present on the face. Though McDonald was wary—and rightly so—of over-deduction, it is obvious from what he said that these signs pointed to a sitting or lying position, with the head lolling forward; the fact that he admitted the possibility of the coroner's theory being correct does not mean that he considered it likely.

Mr Dodds sought only to explain the presence of the most severe area of burning at the front of the middle part of the body and of the scattered burns above the breast. In order to accept Mr Dodds's hypothesis as to the cause of the most severe area of burning (accidental spilling of petrol on the front of the skirt), it is necessary to believe that a girl who had every reason to appreciate the danger was recklessly careless both in handling the can of petrol and in setting fire to the car; there are, however, no provisos to the hypothesis that if the petrol had been poured over her when she was sitting, some of it would have formed a pool in her lap. As for Mr Dodds's notion that the burns above the breast could have been caused by the ignition of petrol which had splashed *upwards* from the can and *towards the body* of Evelyn Foster when she was throwing petrol into the back of the car, one can only say that any theory that needs to argue with a natural law should contain some data to support the alleged aberration.

## 2 The absence of visible signs of bruising

Evelyn Foster said that the man 'knocked her about'; her statement made it clear that she 'became unconscious' as soon as the car was set alight. The coroner inferred a cause-and-effect relationship between the violence and the unconsciousness—but in doing so, he ignored those parts of the statement which showed that, following the violence, the girl was conscious while the man was 'interfering' with her, when the petrol was thrown over her, and when the car 'went up in a blaze'.

Though one cannot completely rule out the possibility that the unconsciousness was a delayed reaction to the blows, the far more obvious inference is that Evelyn Foster fainted from shock, terror, or the sudden intense pain from the burning. Assuming that she told the truth about what happened, and that she was 'knocked about' but not knocked unconscious, it is not at all surprising that no bruising was visible on the 'swollen and obscured' features of her face.

According to Mrs Foster's recollection, Evelyn said that the man 'kept on nipping her arm'. Mr Dodds took 'nipping' to mean pinching, and by a question to Professor McDonald, insinuated to the jury that the apparent absence of bruises on the arms showed that no nipping/pinching had occurred. Of course, even if the coroner's interpretation of the word was correct, the man would have had to exert very strong pressure between his fingers and thumb to cause bruising through the sleeve of both a tweed overcoat and a thick jersey. But if Evelyn Foster did mean that she was continually *pinched*, why on earth did she not use that word instead of the far less colloquially appropriate one? Following the inquest, articles discussing the evidence appeared in several newspapers, and in one such article (oddly enough, by a journalist called Trevor Pinch), the nipping-means-pinching assumption was convincingly contradicted:

> You will remember that the man, in the earlier stages of the tragedy, was sitting next to her while she drove the car, and that she stated he crept, or edged, along the seat towards her. I believe that she meant, in using the word 'nipped', that he wedged her left arm against her side or the back of the seat with his right arm. Is not that equivalent to her arm being 'nipped'? If that is so—and I submit it is highly probable—the significance of the pathological evidence on this point is destroyed.[8]

### 3 Sexual 'interference'

Again, a crucial question concerned the meaning of a word. The word was not used by Evelyn but by Mrs Foster: 'I asked her what happened in the back of the car—had he interfered with her? She replied: "Yes, Mother." ' By 'interference', Mrs Foster meant rape—and she was convinced that her daughter understood it in that way. Perhaps she was right, but it has to be said, first, that she must have thought she knew the answer before she asked the question; second, that she must have *needed* to believe the worst if only to give some sort of meaning to her daughter's death and the savage manner of it; thirdly, that though to her the euphemism had an exact meaning, to Evelyn it could have meant either rape or attempted rape.

A maxim of forensic science is that if the investigator does not know what he is likely to find, he is unlikely to find it. No forensic pathologist would argue with the assertion that, in cases of alleged rape, 'a history of the alleged offence in detail with the facts leading up to it should be elicited'[9]—yet Professor McDonald blithely told the coroner, in so many words, that he had not bothered to find out exactly what Evelyn Foster had said in her statement. This must throw doubt on his findings.

It appears from his report that he did not examine for signs of rape or attempted rape, but only to establish whether or not Evelyn Foster was a virgin. In answer to a question from Mr Smirk, he said: 'The appearances that I found were in every respect compatible with virginity'— which is not the same as saying that she was definitely a virgin. One wonders what appearances he found. The principle signs of virginity are (a) an intact hymen, (b) a normal condition of the fourchette and posterior commissure, (c) a narrow vagina with rugose (wrinkled) walls. One of these signs, or even two, cannot be regarded as evidence of virginity; all three signs must be found. Since, in the case of Evelyn Foster, first-degree burns affected the whole area of external examination, to the extent of exposing bone and muscle, it can be said with virtual certainty that Professor McDonald's opinion was based only on the appearance of the vagina. His opinion did not merely lack sufficient foundation: it lacked any foundation at all.

The final witness was William Jennings, the motor engineer, who described his examination of the car and of the ground at Wolf's Nick. He said that he was satisfied that 'the fire did not result from a leaking petrol pipe, a short circuit, or a silencer explosion', but was caused by 'some agency outside the car itself'.

He gave his opinion that 'the car left the road at an angle of 45 degrees and travelled on the moorland at a speed of about ten miles per hour; had the car travelled faster when it left the road, I would have expected it to go on its nose and turn over; even at that low speed, but for a jutting piece of limestone, the car would have been in danger of overturning'. Jennings appears to have believed that by explaining why the car must have travelled at a low speed when it went down the embankment, he also gave a reason for his opinion that it travelled equally slowly during the rest of its journey. His logic may have been muddled, but at least he made an attempt to explain an opinion. It was the only attempt he made. The rest of his several inferences were given without explanation. For example:

'I inferred that the car travelled under its own power, in low gear, with someone at the steering wheel. I inferred that someone lost interest in driving just before it stopped.'

The coroner drew Jennings's attention to the passage in Evelyn Foster's statement relating to the drive back from Belsay:

'She said he took hold of the steering wheel and drove to Wolf's Nick. What do you say as to the possibility of that—she being on his right, and he driving what must have been a distance of twelve miles?'

'I should say it would be a very difficult thing to do even if she acquiesced and permitted him to drive without resistance. It would be almost an impossibility if she resisted.'

When Mr Bates rose to examine, he concentrated on this last answer:

'The left-hand edge of the steering wheel is almost in the centre of the car?'

Jennings consulted the manual for the Hudson Super-Six, and had to admit that this was so: 'Twenty-one inches against twenty-two and a half inches.'

'You maintain that there is insufficient room for a person to be on the right-hand [sic: left-hand] side of the driver and to allow this person a controlling position if there is no resistance?'

'The person at the wheel would have to get well up to the right-hand side of the car, and the person attempting to drive would have to lean well over.'

'A comparatively experienced driver could drive like that?'

'Yes,' Jennings said, then sought to dilute the affirmation by adding: 'but it would not be by any means safe.'

No further questions: not of this witness nor of any other. The motor engineer left the stand and escorted the jury outside the hall to the courtyard beside the Percy Arms, where a Hudson Super-Six of the same year as Evelyn Foster's was parked. During the few minutes while the members of the jury were examining the car, there was a loud buzz of conversation in the hall. Only two small groups of people did not join in: on one side, Captain Fullarton James and his men, on the other, the Foster family.

By quarter to three, the members of the jury were back in their seats, waiting for Mr Dodds to begin the summing-up.

Murder; suicide; accidental death. These were the alternative solutions to the mystery of Wolf's Nick. But right at the start of the summing-up, Mr Dodds, in his wisdom, advised the jury to discount the suicide theory. He gave no explanation, but simply said:

'Crimes are committed in very many ways; sometimes for obvious reasons, sometimes for reasons unknown. In this case we are dealing with the question as to whether somebody was implicated—a stranger —or whether the deceased herself did it. Subject to what your opinion is, I think we can eliminate any question of suicide.'

There were, said Mr Dodds, two main points for the jury to consider:

'Was the girl murdered? Or did she set fire to the car and in so doing obtain the burns accidentally? If you can answer one of those questions, you will have got an answer to the case.

'If a man was concerned in this case—without knowing who he was —he appears to me to be a homicidal maniac. Either that, or he was doing something to hide something of his own actions.'

Two sentences: thirty-six words. That was the extent of Mr Dodds's discussion of the murder theory. From now on, for over an hour, everything that he said was intended to convince the jury that the accident theory was correct.

First of all, what motive could Evelyn Foster have had for setting fire to the car?

'Might it have been to obtain money from the insurance?' Mr Dodds asked. After telling the jury that he wanted them to be perfectly clear about the terms of the relevant policy, he proceeded to make the terms *unclear* by saying that the policy 'covers cars below 30 hp in [*rather than 'up to'*] the sum of £700 when they take fire outside'. He went on: 'As Mr Foster said in his evidence, this car was included in that policy. In that case, there would be a pecuniary benefit if the girl wanted to burn the car and receive the insurance money.'

If the monetary motive did not appeal to the jury, then 'there are cases where a person becomes obsessed, for some inexplicable reason, with the idea either of gaining notoriety or of doing something abnormal'. Mr Dodds went no further with this line of thought—perhaps because he suddenly remembered that in the formal preamble to the summing-up he had warned the jury that they had to decide the case upon 'the facts as disclosed by the evidence'.

Starting his analysis of the evidence, Mr Dodds drew attention to something that struck him as being 'a little odd' in Evelyn Foster's account of her meeting with the man at Elishaw:

'According to the deceased, the man came down from Jedburgh with some people—he does not call them friends. He appears to have met these people at Jedburgh. He has tea with them. He tells them that he is going to Newcastle, and they say they are going to Hexham. If the story is true, I cannot understand why they did not continue their friendship by giving the man a lift to Hexham. There he would have been more certain of a connection either by train or by bus. At Elishaw he appears to have been left with a definite uncertainty of being able to proceed from there to Newcastle by bus.'

Mr Dodds then referred to three 'extraordinary features' of the evidence relating to the brief period after Evelyn Foster's return from Rochester: first, although Maughan and Thompson 'saw the girl's car outside her father's garage . . . in that circumscribed and small area [they] saw no one get out of the car and walk up the village'; second, although the man was supposed to have gone to the Percy Arms to ask about a lift, and Evelyn Foster was supposed to have met him there, neither of them was seen by the two people serving in the bars at that time; third, 'although it was not usual for Miss Foster to go on long journeys alone with strangers, she did so that night—this despite the fact that her friend Phillipson was available'.

After reminding the jury that the only witness to say that he had definitely seen the Hudson on the road to Newcastle was John Robson, and that the bus driver had estimated the car's speed as no more than ten miles an hour—'which does not seem like a car hurrying with a passenger'—Mr Dodds attacked the evidence of John Kennedy, describing the road mender as 'a man of remarkable views', and pointing out that 'only after he had been recalled did he say, for the first time, that the man driving the car which he says he saw was sitting more sideways than straight on at the wheel; this is in accordance with evidence given earlier—but not by him'. (The suggestion that Kennedy's evidence on recall was perjured was only valid if there was no reference to the driver's position in Kennedy's statement to the police. If there was no such reference, it is difficult to understand why Mr Smirk did not raise the point when he examined the witness the second time; just two questions—'Did you mention the position of the driver in your statement?' followed by 'Why not?'—would have impaired, perhaps destroyed, Kennedy's credibility as a witness.)

Mr Dodds did not think it necessary to read aloud Kennedy's statement (a copy of which must have been among the papers in front of him); on the other hand, he considered Mrs Foster's statement so vital that he read it to the jury not just once but twice. He then stressed 'the fact' that Mrs Foster 'was emphatic that her daughter had said that she was outraged' and compared this with Professor McDonald's evidence that there was no interference. Later, he linked this comparison with others;

'Talking to her mother, the girl made allegations of outrage, nips, and being struck—but could anything be more conclusive than Professor McDonald's report that there were no nips, that there was no violence and, above all, that the girl was a virgin?'

Nearing the end of his survey of 'oddities and extraordinary features', Mr Dodds said that the inference from Evelyn Foster's statement was that the fire started when the car was on the road—yet the evidence of Inspector Russell and William Jennings was that 'there was no fire before the car stopped on the moor'. He invited the jury to draw 'some conclusion' from the evidence that the cap of the petrol can was taken off before the fire. And, last of all, he suggested that 'the position of the burns [were] consistent with the person burned having poured petrol from a can'. This conclusion, he thought, was supported *particularly* both by the presence of burns above the breast ( he was speaking of the localised burns that would seem to have required the petrol to defy the law of gravitation if the can was wielded by Evelyn Foster) and by the fact that, while the left foot was hardly affected by the fire, there were 'superficial burns and blisters' on the right. (Just how this latter point supported the conclusion is anyone's guess. In his theory-outlining question to Professor McDonald, Mr Dodds needed to picture Evelyn Foster with her legs apart when she threw petrol into the car and when she ignited it, thus providing a possible explanation for the severe burns on the inside of the thighs. He therefore postulated that her *left* foot would have been on the running board—where it was far more likely to have been splashed with petrol and exposed to flames shooting through the doorway than the right foot. Perhaps in his own mind Mr Dodds had an explanation for the apparent inconsistency between what he said in his question to the pathologist and what he told the jury—if not, then this was a case of a theorist about a right foot not remembering what the left foot was doing.)

Mr Dodds was stating the obvious—indeed, understating it—when, after closing his manilla folder of notes, he told the jury:

'My opinion, I must say, is that I do not think there is sufficient evidence to say that these burns were caused by another person.' He continued: 'It is for you to decide, of course—but it will be entirely improper for you to say that these burns were caused by another person unless you are absolutely certain that they were so caused.'

Now his tone changed; he was talking of what to him seemed implausible alternatives to the verdict of accidental death:

'On the other hand, it would be equally improper for you to say that the burns were caused in the way I have suggested they might have been, by her setting fire to the car and becoming accidentally alight, unless you were satisfied that that was the cause.

'If you cannot come to a decision as to how these burns were caused, and think the evidence not definite enough, it is open to you to say that you consider there is not sufficient evidence to say definitely how the burns were caused. However, that is a matter for you, and I ask you to retire.'

It was quarter-past four when the jury filed into the small room behind the stage. As soon as the door was closed and a constable stationed beside it, Mr Dodds walked across to the Percy Arms for tea; so did Mr Smirk and Captain Fullarton James and his party. The reporters for the evening papers ran to telephone accounts of the after-lunch proceedings to their offices, one using the telephone at the Percy Arms, two others going to the post office where, in the absence of Stanley Potts on jury duty, Mrs Potts was in charge.

Few, if any, of the spectators left the hall. Within seconds of the coroner's exit, dozens of impromptu discussion groups had formed; the people sitting closest to the Fosters either sat as silent as the family or spoke in whispers, but those sitting towards the back of the hall were unrestrained in their talk. Though there was plenty of argument about the content of the summing-up, no one disagreed with the view that the jury, having been given an unequivocal direction as to what their verdict should be, would not be out for long.

But an hour passed: longer than anyone had expected. The caretaker put a match to his light-pole and went round the hall, jerking the chains on the acetylene lamps and firing the gas within the lacy white cups. Yet another hour went by. Then, at twenty minutes past six, the door of the small room opened and George MacDougall, the foreman of the jury, spoke to the constable outside. The door was closed again. Another constable hurried across to the Percy Arms to fetch the coroner, the senior police officers and Mr Smirk.

The jury returned to their seats at 6.25. The fizzing of the acetylene jets, the squeak of a chair as someone craned forward: for a moment these were the only sounds in the hall.

Mr Dodds turned to face the jury. His voice sounded unnaturally loud as he put the formal question:

'Are you agreed upon your verdict, gentlemen?'

MacDougall stood up. He was holding a slip of paper, but he did not look at it as he replied:

'Yes, Mr Dodds. The verdict is wilful murder against some person unknown.'

According to the reporter for the *Newcastle Daily Journal*, 'the coroner appeared somewhat surprised'. A murmur went up from the spectators, and two or three people standing in the porch clapped their hands.

Mr Dodds shook his head slightly—whether to clear it or to signify his disagreement with the verdict does not appear from the reports. 'I suppose you mean that somebody deliberately poured petrol over her and set her on fire?'

'Yes,' MacDougall said.

Mr Dodds rephrased the verdict in official terms, reading the words aloud as he wrote:

'We, the jury, find that Evelyn Foster died on the 7th day of January, 1931, at The Kennels, Otterburn, from shock due to burns caused by petrol being wilfully thrown over her and ignited by some person or some persons unknown.'

MacDougall nodded. 'That is correct.'

'Well, that concludes the hearing,' Mr Dodds said bleakly. He was already collecting his papers together, using them as an excuse for not looking at the jury, as he added: 'Thank you, gentlemen.'

The reporter for the *North Mail* noted that 'Mrs Foster, with tears welling in her eyes and showing obvious signs of the ordeal through which she had passed, was one of the first to leave the hall'. Joseph, who also was crying, tried to catch up with his wife, but the way was blocked by newspapermen and by friends wanting to shake hands with him. Asked about the verdict, he said: 'It is what I expected. I don't think the jury could do anything else. The verdict vindicates my daughter. There is great relief in knowing that it is all over.'

Other reporters sought a comment from Captain Fullarton James as he marched from the hall to his dented car, but he pushed them aside, saying that he did not consider it proper to express an opinion on the case.

As it turned out, the chief constable's words were not strictly true. What he really meant was that he did not consider it proper to express an opinion at that particular moment or to those particular reporters.

The front page of the following morning's *Daily Express* carried a story by Leslie Randall, the newspaper's crime correspondent. The salient feature of the story was a statement attributed to Captain Fullarton James which, if correctly reported, meant that the Northumberland County Constabulary discounted the inquest jury's verdict as being against the weight of the evidence:

'We are satisfied that the motor car in which Miss Foster's supposed murderer is said to have travelled from Jedburgh does not exist. We are also satisfied that the man she described does not exist.'

Even close acquaintances of Captain Fullarton James could not believe that his megalomania had led him to employ the royal plural form; therefore, his use of the word 'we' showed that he was speaking, not personally, but on behalf of the police force. What the statement said, in effect, was that the Northumberland police considered themselves not simply the instruments of law and order: they were also the judges of guilt or innocence, of truth or lie. But had the statement actually been made? Before repeating it in their own columns, the editors of the *Express*'s rivals sent reporters to police headquarters to ask if the chief constable wished to repudiate it. They were told that he had nothing to say on the matter. This, then, seemed to confirm that the statement had been reported accurately. During the day, the police moved out of Otterburn Tower, and an announcement was made that all officers engaged on the case were returning to normal duties in their respective divisions. This was taken to mean that the investigation had ended—that the police had no intention of continuing what they were sure had been a wild-goose chase, a search for a figment of imagination.

The effect of all this on the Foster family must have been profound. At the end of the inquest, Joseph Foster had said: 'There is great relief in knowing that it is all over.' But now it turned out that the only thing that was over was the investigation. Now there were two opposing verdicts: that of the jury and that of the police. It was up to the public to decide which verdict to accept.

On the Friday, none of the family would talk to reporters, but the *Evening World*'s 'special correspondent in Otterburn' achieved a small scoop by persuading a member of the jury to comment on the chief constable's statement:[10]

> Surely we were in the best position to form an accurate judgment in the case? We listened hour after hour to the evidence. We sifted every little detail, and we, of course, knew something of the sterling character of the poor girl herself.
>
> We are certainly surprised to see that there is an attempt to dispute our finding that Miss Foster was murdered.
>
> It is preposterous to suggest that a dying girl, suffering the agony that Evelyn Foster must have suffered, would readily invent such a convincing story as the one she told on her death-bed. It may be true that a certain amount of the expert evidence was against the murder theory. But you can produce expert evidence to support almost any theory, and we jurymen decided on our verdict—as we were bound to do—by the use of common-sense and the careful examination of every fact placed before us by the witnesses.

On the Saturday morning, the family's silence was broken by Joseph Foster, who told reporters who came to The Kennels: 'We find it difficult to believe that a man of the chief constable's experience and standing and official position would say such a thing. He must either accept the verdict of the jury or take steps to secure a second inquest.' Joseph said that he intended to seek legal advice (Mr Bates's name was not mentioned in this regard), and added that he would be writing to

Colonel Douglas Clifton Brown, the local member of parliament,[11] with the aim of having the matter raised in the House of Commons.

Two *Evening World* reporters decided to anticipate events by ascertaining the MP's response to a letter that was still to be written. Posing as emissaries of the Foster family, they obtained an interview with Colonel Brown at his home, Ruffside Hall, near Consett, County Durham. His replies to their questions were reported as follows in late editions of the evening paper:

> Questioned as to the possibility of the matter of the Chief Constable's alleged statement being raised in Parliament, Colonel Brown said that it had already occurred to him that it was possibly his duty to raise the matter in the House of Commons.
>
> 'In any event,' he said, 'I am sure that somebody or other will carry the matter farther. It is not likely that it will be allowed to pass.
>
> 'As I have already indicated, I think strongly on the matter, and further, when you now tell me that the parents are sending a letter of appeal to me as their Member of Parliament, I shall consider very carefully and seriously whether it is my duty to raise the matter in the House of Commons. Indeed, I think it is both necessary and desirable from the public point of view that the matter should be taken up.
>
> 'At any rate, there will be no difficulty in wording a question that will be satisfactory to all. At the same time, I personally am placed in a very difficult position because of my friendship with the Chief Constable.'

Despite the undergrowth of politicians' stock phrases, the style of which is one of the few things that remain unchanged in a changing world, the message was clear: if 'somebody or other' did not accept Colonel Brown's responsibility, and he was forced to table a question in the House, his main concern would be to frame it in such a way that neither the question nor the answer embarrassed his friend and fellow ex-officer, Captain Fullarton James. A cursory reading between the lines of the report of the interview convinced Joseph Foster that the most he could expect from his elected representative was the least he wanted. Deciding to write direct to the Home Secretary, J. R. Clynes, he enlisted the assistance of his wife and daughters in composing a letter which was posted on Tuesday, 10 February, and which read, in part:

> Sir,
>
> May I respectfully call your attention to the extraordinary and unprecedented position that exists following the Coroner's inquiry into the death of my daughter, Evelyn Foster? . . .
>
> The jury returned a verdict that my daughter was murdered by some

person or persons unknown. Many painful and scandalous innuendoes against my daughter's character were made during the inquest. It was even suggested that she had fired her car herself to obtain the insurance money, although no one pointed out that insurance companies settle a claim on the market value of the car, and not on the sum for which it is insured. It was also suggested that my daughter may have set fire to the car to gain notoriety for herself. There was not a tittle of evidence to support these shameful theories, but I recognise that they were perhaps inevitable, distressing though they were to my family. The jury's verdict vindicated my girl's integrity and good faith.

My family, however, was not to be spared another public attack on my daughter's honesty. The Chief Constable of Northumberland, in an interview with a newspaper man—an interview he has not repudiated—is credited with the statement that the inquest verdict was against the weight of evidence, and that my girl was not murdered.

Surely I am entitled to protest vigorously against this kind of apology [sic]? The police force must, no doubt, protect itself from public distrust when a crime remains unsolved, but I resent the police force covering its own failures through a veiled and uncalled-for attack on my dead daughter.

This is a matter to which I earnestly hope and pray you will devote your attention, in conjunction with the following questions:—

1. Was my daughter's burned car left unprotected for hours so that finger-prints could not be taken?

2. Is it also a fact that the police made no attempt to check footprints on the scene of the tragedy until the ground had been trampled over by curious spectators?

3. Why was the skill and experience of Scotland Yard ignored by the Northumberland Police?

We have suffered a great bereavement and personal shock that will remain with us to the end of our days. All I can do now is to defend my daughter's honour along lines which may protect other parents from the painful procedure to which Mrs Foster and myself have been subjected.

I remain, Sir,
Your obedient servant,

J. J. FOSTER

A fortnight later, on 24 February, Joseph received a note signed by Sir Ernley Blackwell, the Under-Secretary at the Home Office:

If you consider that you have a complaint against the Chief Constable of the Northumberland County Police Force, you should bring the matter to the notice of the Northumberland Standing Joint Committee, the police authority for the county.

The Fosters felt that putting the complaint to the local police authority would be rather like asking a Bench of Bishops to adjudicate on whether Jesus Christ was the son of God. But as there appeared to be no alternative, a copy was made of the letter to the Home Secretary and of Sir Ernley Blackwell's reply, and these were sent with a covering note to Alderman Thomas Taylor, the chairman of the committee.

Though the reason for the Fosters' pessimism may have been unfounded, the result of the 'inquiry', as it was called, was as they expected. The committee met on Tuesday, 24 March, at the Moot Hall in Newcastle, the headquarters of the administrative staff for Northumberland. The inquiry was held in private, but it is possible to piece together what happened from an interview given by a member of the committee to a reporter for the *Newcastle Evening Chronicle* and from the letter to Joseph Foster, written the same day and signed by the clerk to the county council, in which the committee's findings were set out.

After a few introductory words from the chairman, Captain Fullarton James presented a report to the committee. This began:

> With regard to the paragraph in Mr J. J. Foster's letter to the Secretary of State alleging that I made a statement on the verdict of the coroner's jury to a newspaper reporter, I wish to say that no such statement was made. I did, however, have what I considered a confidential conversation with a reporter about two hours before the jury returned their verdict.[12] I had no idea the conversation would be published, and I complained to the editor of the newspaper in question immediately I saw a paragraph in it which purported to set out a summary of the conversation.

Referring to the last of Joseph Foster's three specific questions, the chief constable merely said that he had not considered it necessary to obtain assistance from Scotland Yard.

He made no reference to the allegations regarding finger-prints and footprints, but gave the following explanation for the fact that the scene of the crime was left unprotected:

> The nearest officer was stationed six miles away. When the matter was brought to his notice, more important steps than the setting of a guard on the car demanded to be taken immediately. A guard was placed on the car at the earliest practicable moment.

Last of all, the chief constable said that there was no truth in the suggestion that the investigation had been abandoned:

> The police will pursue every line of inquiry likely to lead to a solution of the problems raised by the death of Miss Evelyn Foster. A number of new lines of inquiry are being and have been investigated.[13]

Captain Fullarton James was not exactly inundated with questions when he came to the end of the reading. It appears that there was just one: If he did not believe that a murder had been committed, why were inquiries being continued?

'My duty offers no alternative,' he answered, 'no matter what personal theories investigations have led me to form.'

Stirred by this reply, a member started to move a vote of confidence, but was interrupted by the chairman, who ruled that such a vote would be 'wholly superfluous':

'There is no suggestion that our confidence in the chief constable has been shaken. Furthermore, we are satisfied that in the emergency and unusual circumstances, the police conducted their investigations in a proper manner.'

And that was that. The chairman's words were greeted with a unanimous chorus of 'hear-hears' and, there being no further business, tea and biscuits were served to the members and the man whose actions had supposedly been under their scrutiny.

The announcement of the findings created considerable discussion in Northumberland. It is impossible to say what the majority view was, but in and around Otterburn the general feeling was that there had been a 'white-wash job'.

This may have been too harsh a judgement; all one can say for certain is that the committee was not the most searching of tribunals. The members may have been right to accept without question the chief constable's assertions regarding the time and the circumstances of his conversation with Leslie Randall; and, from a practical point of view, they had no choice but to support his decision not to call in Scotland Yard. But their acceptance of his explanation for the delay in placing a guard at Wolf's Nick can only be ascribed to mass gullibility or a gritting-the-teeth determination to accept whatever he told them, no matter how absurd.

Captain Fullarton James's statement that 'the nearest officer was stationed six miles away' was completely irrelevant (it was also untrue: a constable was stationed at Kirkwhelpington). By midnight, Andrew Fergusson had been joined by Sergeant Shanks and Constable Proud; Fergusson had telephoned a report to Superintendent Shell at Hexham, and details of the case had been passed to police headquarters at Morpeth. It was arrant nonsense to suggest, as the chief constable did, that the Otterburn village policeman was the only officer who could have arranged for the scene of the crime to be guarded. Equally nonsensical, and just as obviously so, was the assertion that the 'earliest practicable moment' for this to be done was some eight hours after the start of the investigation. Even if it had been true that the village constable was the only officer required to make decisions that night, with everyone else blindly following his orders and not daring even to suggest higher priorities in his plan of action, the 'more important steps' that 'demanded to be taken immediately' must have been accomplished hours before the allegedly less important step of placing a guard at Wolf's Nick was taken. The obvious truth of the matter—made more obvious by the fact that three policemen visited Wolf's Nick at one o'clock in the morning and left half an hour or so later—is that not until some time after six o'clock did it occur to anyone that the scene of the crime should be, and should have been, protected.

Significantly, the committee's letter to Joseph Foster made no mention of the chief constable's explanation (no, let us call it what it was—a feeble excuse) for the delay.

The uninquisitive inquiry can be said to mark the end of the Foster case. For months afterwards, Joseph and Gordon Foster and a 'committee of friends' sought evidence to confirm the jury's verdict, but none of the information they passed on to the police caused any observable response.

Directly after the inquiry, Captain Fullarton James gave verbal instructions that if the incident at Wolf's Nick *had* to be referred to, then it was not to be called a 'case'; the collections of witness statements, reports, and press cuttings were deposited in fresh folders labelled THE FOSTER AFFAIR. The chief constable, secure in the belief that he had done nothing wrong and that his officers had done everything right, made what he thought was a joke when the new folders were shewn to him. 'The affair is over,' he said. 'I was never particularly attracted to the girl anyway.'

1  In 1931 the theory lacked adequate research support, but post-war research tends to confirm it; see, eg, Morton, J. H., and others (1953), *Am. J. Obstet. Gynec.*, 65, 1182; Mandell, A. J., and Mandell, M. P. (1967), *J. Am. Med. Ass.*, 200, 792; Hands, J., and others (1974), *Med. Sci. Law*, 14, 35; Scutt, J. A. (1974), *Criminol.*, 9, 34, 56.

2  For the mechanically-minded reader, the specifications of the Hudson Super-Six are set out in the Appendix.

3  Kirsopp-Reid was a Northumberland County Councillor; his visit to Newcastle may have been to attend a council meeting at the Moot Hall.

4  Ernest Bates afterwards caused his own downfall by becoming involved with certain corrupt local politicians. He was, perhaps, what might be called 'geographically unfortunate': though the incidence of corruption is no higher in north-eastern politics and local government than elsewhere in the country, the criminals are more often found out.

5  It appears that only the neck of the can was produced to the witness; presumably, in order to examine the inside of the can, someone connected with the investigation had sawn off the neck. Though the can itself must have been an exhibit, it is not referred to as such in any reports of the inquest.

6  For the benefit of readers who have forgotten pre-decimalisation coins, the half-crown was about $1\frac{1}{4}$in in diameter.

7  Bruce Jupp, of the Petroleum Industry Training Board, contends that no expert—as opposed to expert witness—would venture an opinion on this question, since speed of evaporation is regulated by a number of factors, the most important being the *amount* of petrol.

8  *Sunday Sun*, 8 February 1931.

9  *Practical Forensic Medicine*, Camps, F. E., and Cameron, J. M., Hutchinson 1971.

10  The juryman was not identified in the report, but was almost certainly Vicar Brierley.

11  Colonel Brown was MP for Hexham 1918–23 and 1924–51. He was Speaker of the House of Commons from 1943 until 1951, when he was created 1st Viscount Ruffside of Hexham.

12  Or, to put it another way, just after the jury retired.

13  Perhaps it was a coincidence that there was more police activity in Otterburn in the three days before the committee met than in the whole of the previous six weeks. The *Newcastle Evening Chronicle* reported:

> Sergeant Shanks, from Bellingham, visited Otterburn on Saturday and made new inquiries, including a call on the Foster family. Then, on Sunday, a police party headed by Superintendent Spratt, from Alnwick, came into the village. This activity and other signs of investigation have satisfied Mr Foster that the hunt to clear up his daughter's death is going on unabated—indeed, with renewed vigour. 'The police have told me that they are going on with the search,' he said. . . . 'I wish I knew what has changed their minds.'

# 6

*Every problem becomes very childish when once it is explained to you.*

I cannot recall when or where I first read about the burning of Evelyn Foster, but the case began to exert a fascination during the early days of my research for a book on the Wallace murder case. While looking through the yellowing newspapers of January and February 1931 for accounts of the Liverpool case, I was often side-tracked by piquant headlines referring to THE RIDDLE OF THE OTTERCOPS, THE WOLF'S NICK MYSTERY, THE OTTERBURN PUZZLE.

A year or so later, my wife and I stopped at Otterburn on our way to Edinburgh, and I experienced a feeling almost of déjà vu, for the village was virtually as I had pictured it from the old newspaper reports. The imagined reality of what a place used to be like is often more real than the reality of what the place has become, but Otterburn had a truer existence in relation to the Foster case than the sort of film-set street-scene, made up only of façades, that I had constructed in my mind. All the landmarks were there: Otterburn Tower, the Percy Arms, the War Memorial Hall, The Kennels, even Foster's Garage. And, of course, farther along the road, unsurprisingly unchanged, was Elishaw.

Perhaps some day, I thought, I'll try to write a book about the Foster case.

Two years after that first brief visit, we went back to Otterburn; we stayed there this time, at the Otterburn Tower Hotel. I had decided to write this book, and during the previous month or so had read a number of articles and essays on the case. My 'homework' had led me to believe that, for a change, I would not be writing about a murder. Despite having read Julian Symons's excellent essay, 'The Invisible Man',[1] with its impressive arguments in support of the theory that Evelyn Foster was murdered, I had formed the strong opinion that she had caused her own death.

But this opinion was less strong when I returned home. I had a mass of notes of interviews with people who were connected with the Foster case, or who simply remembered it, or who remembered their parents talking about it. Though none of the things I had been told was particularly significant on its own, some of them formed a synergy, a sum greater than its parts, which suggested that Evelyn Foster's story may have been true.

I visited Otterburn on other occasions during the following months, and corresponded or talked with members of the medical profession, motor engineers, veteran-car enthusiasts, serving and retired policemen, expatriates of Northumberland. Information obtained earlier was sometimes confirmed, sometimes contradicted; new facts came to light; comments that had seemed irrelevant when they were made acquired a meaning when linked with others.

By the time I started writing this book, my early opinion about the case had been reversed: I was convinced that the evidence disclosed by the police did not justify the belief that Evelyn Foster's death was the result of suicide or accident—and, more important, it appeared to me that facts which the police either did not know or did not divulge strongly supported her account of what happened on that Twelfth Night of 1931.

I have already discussed most of the evidence that was offered at the inquest; some of the undisclosed evidence, too. Of the few things that remain to be said, there are one or two which I believe change the probability that Evelyn Foster was murdered into virtual certainty.

Every member of the jury had known Evelyn Foster. At the start of the inquest, most, if not all, of them believed that she had been murdered. But this does not mean that they closed their minds to the evidence. There is no reason to believe that they would not have altered their preconceived verdict if they had considered that the evidence went against it. Several reports of the proceedings refer to the apparent conscientiousness of the jury, and three days after the inquest, the reporter for the *Sunday Sun* observed:

I know there has been a disposition to suggest that the jury were influenced by a feeling of local patriotism; I saw no indication of such suasion. They gave due attention to every witness and to every detail. Each of the nine men made copious notes of points in the evidence. The Vicar, the Rev. J. P.

B. Brierley, who was one of them, filled about a score of foolscap sheets with notes.

The length of their deliberations is a further indication of conscientiousness. But perhaps the strongest indication of all is the known fact that, having discarded the accident theory, they ignored Mr Dodds's advice and discussed the possibility of suicide. It was a natural progression. None of the jurymen was impressed by the coroner's suggestion that Evelyn Foster might have set fire to the car with the intention of defrauding the insurance company; on the other hand, there was unanimous agreement that Professor McDonald's evidence regarding the burns on the body provided near-conclusive proof that the girl was sitting in the back of the car when the fire started, and that this ruled out the accident theory. Was it possible, though, that Mr Dodds's suggestion that Evelyn Foster might have become 'obsessed, for some inexplicable reason, with the idea either of gaining notoriety or of doing something abnormal' could be applied to suicide by burning? Was it possible that she had decided to take her own life, and had invented the story of the passenger as a means of disguising suicide as murder?

In seeking answers to these questions, the jury's knowledge of Evelyn Foster was invaluable; indeed, without such knowledge, they could not have attempted to answer them. Mr Dodds's instruction that they had to 'judge upon the facts as disclosed by the evidence' was negated by his telling them that they might consider whether Evelyn Foster was mentally abnormal. Since no evidence was given concerning the girl's personality, the jury had to judge upon the facts as they knew them.

But none of the nine men knew—or had even picked up from village gossip—anything that suggested that Evelyn Foster was not a sane and happy person. The vicar afterwards told his son Peter: 'I would stake my reputation as a parish priest who knows his people that she was not the kind of girl who would commit suicide.'

There is a saying that no one suddenly becomes a murderer. One could say with at least as much assurance that no one suddenly becomes suicidal. If Evelyn Foster showed any signs of a self-destructive urge, they were not observed or recognised as such by people who were in daily contact with her.

Seeking to remedy the absence of expert psychiatric evidence at the inquest, I gave identical reports of the case to two psychiatrists and asked for their views on whether suicide was a feasible theory. One replied, in part:

> From such as I could glean, the likely explanation of the case is that the girl deliberately used the car as a funeral pyre for herself, only shortly afterwards to recant as death was not instantaneous. Her motivation for such behaviour would involve emotional instability, sexual anxieties and an active phantasy life. Her detailed account of her assailant and his actions would fit this picture, as would her desire to blame a man and not herself for what occurred.

The other psychiatrist had this to say:

> It seems to me that there is really no adequate evidence to suggest that this unfortunate woman committed suicide. Although I have no direct clinical experience of this,[2] I should have thought that people who commit suicide in such a spectacular and unpleasant way are always suffering from serious psychiatric disorder. One would expect that a few may be early or borderline schizophrenics who may commit suicide in a bizarre fashion, the method of suicide being possibly related to delusional thinking. Others may perhaps be suffering from a serious depressive illness. However, the majority are probably people with gross hysterical-personality disorders, who would have a long history of seriously unstable behaviour. Such a person may be more inclined to commit such an act in front of an audience rather than on a lonely road by night. On the evidence available, I think one must assume that this was in fact a case of murder and not of suicide.

Clearly, unless the reader has faith in the coin-tossing or eeny-meeny-miny-mo methods of choosing between contradictory conclusions, both of these diagnoses must be ignored.

I searched the psychiatric literature for possible 'clues', for symptoms common to many firesetters or to many people who commit suicide by savage means; but without success. The trouble, I found, is that the 'practical' monographs and papers consist almost entirely of case-study material in which the postulated symptoms are so diverse, yet individually are so rarely applicable to more than a comparatively small number of cases, that after a couple of hours' reading one gets the uneasy feeling that most people in the world, oneself included, exhibit some symptom or other.

Though I came across no information that seemed to relate to either the accident or suicide theories in the Foster case, a passage in the most formidable book I read[3] struck me as having a possible bearing on the murder theory. The authors assert that the factor most common among male pyromaniacs is that 'they begin life with an exaggerated wish to become leading participants in the contemporary drama and then, when it is realised fate has relegated them to insignificant roles, they secretly stage a drama of their own, in which they are author, stage director and the leading actor. . . . By a single match they show themselves sufficiently clever to propound a mysterious crime which confounds the "experts" and cause the authorities to seem helpless.'

If one accepts the possibility—and one surely must—that Evelyn Foster's assailant did not achieve a sexual climax from his 'interference' with her, then a later sentence in the same book may also be relevant: 'Most [pyromaniacs] admit to some sort of thwarting in their sexual desires just preceeding the firesetting, but to them the act is not a substitute for sexual gratification, but rather a means whereby they relieve the accumulated rage induced by the frustration.'

Before turning from psychiatric generalisations to facts, it is worth mentioning that a number of authorities contend that the 'imitative syndrome'—which, in simple terms, means that certain people who are both unstable and impressionable tend to copy much-publicised crimes —is especially strong in connection with crimes involving fire. January 1931 is a red-letter month for those whom Sir Leon Radzinowicz calls 'forensic stamp collectors'. As well as the Foster and Wallace cases, there was the murder of Louisa Steele at Blackheath (a crime that was never solved), and in the same month, a reward offered by the *Daily Mail* led to Sarah Hearn being traced and subsequently charged with murdering the wife of a friend by mixing arsenic with tinned salmon in a sandwich. (Although, unlike Major Armstrong's arsenic-tinctured scone, the lethal sandwich was not passed to the victim with a polite 'Excuse fingers,' Mrs Hearn would almost certainly have gone to the gallows had she not been defended by Norman Birkett, who somehow conjured an acquittal from the jury at Bodmin Assizes.)

There was yet another case associated with this particular January. Right at the end of the month, Alfred Arthur Rouse was found guilty at Northampton Assizes of the 'blazing car murder'. The jury can have had little difficulty in deciding that Rouse, wishing to be thought dead but unwilling to accept the inconvenience of dying, had picked up an unknown hitch-hiker on the previous Guy Fawkes Night, driven to the lane leading to the village of Hardingstone, knocked the man unconscious in the front seat and, after soaking the car with petrol, set fire to it. So far as is known, this was the first time that this method of murder was used in this country. Rouse, in addition to being an innovator in the field of homicide, was a sexual prodigy (according to one unsubstantiated estimate, he either put forty women in the family way or was responsible for rather fewer women giving birth to forty illegitimate children), so the case attracted inordinate press coverage.

Does it not seem more than just a coincidence that, only two months after the original 'blazing car murder'—two months during which the name of Rouse was rarely absent from the front pages—there was another case involving a blazing car?

If there had not been a Rouse case, would there have been a Foster case?

It is an intriguing thought—and one that adds a further dimension of horror to the burning of Evelyn Foster—that what happened at Wolf's Nick on Twelfth Night, 1931, may have been inspired by what happened in Hardingstone Lane on Guy Fawkes Night, 1930.[4]

One of the main reasons given for disbelieving Evelyn Foster's story was—and is—that the driver of the car she claimed to have seen at Elishaw never came forward. Despite police appeals on the radio and in the press, the 'mystery woman' remained—well, a mystery. So did the other passenger, or passengers, in the car.

A passage from Mr Dodds's summing-up bears repeating:

> According to the deceased, the man came down from Jedburgh with some people—he does not call them friends. He appears to have met these people at Jedburgh. He has tea with them. He tells them that he is going to Newcastle, and they say they are going to Hexham. If the story is true, I cannot understand why they did not continue their friendship by giving the man a lift to Hexham. There he would have been more certain of a connection either by train or by bus. At Elishaw he appears to have been left with a definite uncertainty of being able to proceed from there to Newcastle by bus.

Something that seems to have escaped Mr Dodds is that Evelyn Foster may have given a true summary of an untrue story. During the drive from Elishaw to Otterburn, the passenger may not have been contemplating any crime more serious than that of gypping a hire-car driver of the fare to Ponteland; even so, it is unlikely that he would have given away information that might afterwards help the police to identify him. His whole story of meeting the people in Jedburgh could have been an invention. (It has to be said, however, that his assertion that he had had tea with the people in Jedburgh was not discounted by the inability of the police to trace any hotel or restaurant employee who remembered such a party:[5] tea could have been taken at a private house.)

Evelyn Foster's account of the meeting at Elishaw seemed to receive support from the evidence of Albert Beach, the steam-roller driver, who claimed that at about ten minutes to seven he saw two cars near Elishaw—the first in Dere Street, heading south towards Hexham, and the second on the road to Otterburn (see page 87). Among the 170 or so people who made statements to the police but were not called as witnesses at the inquest was a gardener named Robert Townes, who lived at Brownrigg Cottages, about half a mile along Dere Street from Elishaw. His statement, giving further credence to the girl's story, was to the effect that he was in Dere Street, close to his home, at ten minutes to seven, that he saw Beach walking along the road, and that at virtually the same time he was passed by 'a touring car with the hood up' travelling from Elishaw, and saw another car, 'which appeared to be a saloon, stop 200 yards on the Otterburn side of the cross-roads and restart a few moments later'. Why the police decided to keep Townes's evidence from the jury is hard to surmise without being rude about them.

In seeking an answer to the question of what happened to the car that went down Dere Street, it appears that one can at once rule out what would, at first sight, seem the most likely possibility. Almost certainly, *the car did not go on to Hexham*—indeed, it apparently did not continue along Dere Street for more than a few miles. The reason for saying this is that at ten minutes to seven a pair of cyclists, a Mr Wallace and a Mr Bell, set off for Rochester from Woodburn, the village bisected by Dere Street, roughly six miles from Elishaw—and did not meet a single vehicle before they reached the Otterburn–Jedburgh road.

The car could only have branched off from Dere Street at a cross-road midway between Elishaw and Woodburn: the left-hand turning leads to the southern end of Otterburn, close by the mill, and the turning on the right is the way to the small town of Bellingham. Since there is no reason to believe that the 'mystery woman' was the murderer's accomplice, there is practically no likelihood that she took the dog-leg route to Otterburn instead of continuing along the road from Jedburgh. It is almost certain, then, that the car either turned right towards Bellingham —*or stopped at a house or farm somewhere along the first couple of miles of Dere Street after Elishaw.*

Consideration of this latter possibility led some people in Otterburn to believe that they knew the identity of the 'mystery woman'. Though the object of their suspicions is now dead, I do not intend to name her but will refer to her as 'Mrs X'. The facts about her, so far as I know them, are as follows:

She lived in one of the few houses on Dere Street between Elishaw and the Otterburn–Bellingham cross-road. The house, which has since been demolished, stood on fourteenth-century foundations and was described in a Northumberland guide-book as 'a solid stone Georgian building, looking like the scene of a Brontë novel'; it is reputed to have been haunted by a canine ghost—a dog that, on and off for five and a half centuries, whimpered for the return of its master, who was killed at the battle of Otterburn.

Mrs X was one of the wealthiest women in the district. Her husband's family owned a large and flourishing cotton firm, the name of which would be recognised by most people who have ever sewn buttons on shirts. Mrs X was about 50 years of age, and she and her husband had been married for nearly 30 years; they had no children.

In 1931, 'two-car families' were few and far between, but Mr and Mrs X each had a car. Towards the end of 1930, after driving a Ford for two or three years, Mrs X bought a new Morris saloon. (Whether Evelyn Foster was aware that Mrs X was driving a different car is not known. The woman rarely patronised Foster's Garage; indeed, she was not often seen in the village, her trips usually taking her either to Jedburgh, to Hexham, or—via the turning off Dere Street coming out by Otterburn Mill—to Newcastle.) Mr X needed a car because he had to make frequent visits to Glasgow on business (he was away from home from the morning of 6 January until the afternoon of the following day)—and Mrs X needed a car, not only for mundane, wifely activities like shopping, but also as an aid to the extra-marital side of what one flinches from calling her 'double-life' but which was, in fact, exactly that. In the presence of her husband, their relatives and their mutal friends, she gave the appearance of being completely satisfied with the life they saw her leading; but when her husband was away, she often held drinking-parties at the house, acting as chauffeuse to guests lacking their own means of transport—or, in the absence of company, either drove to a pub where she thought she was not known or got extremely drunk in her own home.

An odd, perhaps pathetic, sidelight on her solitary domestic drinking sessions is that she sometimes dressed up for them—or, at least, during them—in her by-now-rather-faded wedding gown. Her daily woman, who still lives in Otterburn, recalls occasions when she arrived at the house at an early hour and found Mrs X slumped across the living-room sofa, enveloped in a mist of muslin and lace, with an empty bottle and glass near at hand. The servant would half-carry Mrs X to her bedroom, help her to undress, then fold the wedding gown into a cardboard box that rattled with moth-balls and rustled with tissue paper. Mrs X must have had a built-in alarm-clock, because when her husband returned she was always conventionally dressed, had smothered the smell of gin on her breath with cachous, and had made sure that the daily woman had removed all evidence of the previous night's party or lonely drinking bout.

Perhaps Mrs X was afflicted by *nostalgie de la boue*; perhaps she was so desperate for companionship that she considered any company better than none. Whatever the reason, she numbered among her illicit acquaintances some very low types indeed. The most patently ne'er-do-well of her acquaintances were two brothers—frequent visitors to her house, as she was to their cottage near Jedburgh—who augmented the small sums of money they made from odd-jobbery by poaching, sheep-stealing, and other rural villainies. When under the influence of drink, as they often were, they derived brutish pleasure from picking fights with people in pubs and at dances.

On the morning of Wednesday, 7 January 1931, just a few hours after Evelyn Foster died, Mrs X suddenly developed influenza. So severe was the attack that she felt quite unable to meet the police when they called to ask if she could help with their inquiries regarding a car that had travelled from Elishaw along Dere Street the night before. It is not known whether the police went back to the house after allowing a day or so for her to recover.

Mrs X may have believed that intense cold was a cure for influenza.

There seems only one other possible explanation for her leaving the house twice on the Wednesday, before her husband's return, each time to visit a small but dense plantation of conifers in the grounds—a place that, according to the daily woman's recollection, she had never visited before: a place that would have provided sanctuary for someone hiding from the police.

One person who was convinced that Mrs X was the 'mystery woman' was William Blackham, the village schoolmaster. His daughter, now Mrs Dorothy Groves, recalls that he refused to discuss the Foster case in the presence of his children. However, one day soon after the inquest, Blackham was visited by an old friend, and Dorothy listened outside the door of the living-room as they talked over the evidence. The friend raised the question of the 'mystery woman', and Dorothy heard her father walk across to the window. 'Come here,' he said, and the friend joined him. 'You see that house on the top of the rise?' The friend murmured that he did. 'Well, that is the home of the woman who drove the car. There is no doubt about it in my mind.' The only house that could be seen through the window was across the triangle of fields that separated the Otterburn–Jedburgh road from Dere Street: the home of Mrs X. The conversation between Blackham and his friend continued; but not within earshot of Dorothy, who was caught eavesdropping by her mother and sent off to finish her homework.

The schoolmaster may have had more reasons for being suspicious of Mrs X than I have been able to glean; this appears likely, for he does not seem to have been a man who would have based a firm conclusion on insufficient data. The few facts that I have given suggest the *possibility* that Mrs X was the driver of the car at Elishaw; one can go no farther than that. But if she *was* the driver, then three things are clear:

First, whether she drove the bowler-hatted man from the direction of Jedburgh or from her home, Elishaw was for her the most convenient place to drop him so that he might get a lift to Newcastle. Coming from Jedburgh, Elishaw was the farthest she could take him without going out of her way.

Second, Mrs X knew that Evelyn Foster invariably drove to *and from* Rochester on Tuesday evenings, always leaving Otterburn at the same time—just after the arrival of the bus from Hexham—and, depending on the number of stops to let passengers off, starting the return journey within about twenty minutes. On at least one occasion, presumably when her own car was out of action, Mrs X had travelled on the Hexham market-day bus and afterwards used the 'mini-bus' service to get from Foster's Garage to Elishaw. If Mrs X dropped the man at Elishaw, it was not on the *off-chance* of his getting a lift from there, but *in the knowledge* that Evelyn Foster would be along at any minute and would take him at least as far as Otterburn.

Third, and perhaps most important, Mrs X had good reason to hide her connection with the Foster case. If she had admitted being the driver of the car at Elishaw, she would have had to admit a good many other things as well—not just to the police but to her husband. She would, for instance, have had to implicate the other man—or men—in the car; would have had to explain what she had done during the day and how she had spent the night. The duality of her life, her sordid relationships, her lies—all would have been in peril of exposure. If she even considered responding to the police appeals, she may have decided that she could add little, if anything, to the description of the man given by Evelyn Foster—that, by coming forward, she would confirm the murdered girl's account of the meeting at Elishaw but would contribute nothing towards the apprehension of the criminal. It would have seemed like a straight choice, and a simple one for Mrs X to make, between saving one or other of two reputations: Evelyn Foster's or her own.

Much was made at the time of the case, by those who disbelieved Evelyn Foster's story, of the 'invisibility' of her alleged murderer during the ten minutes or so when he was supposed to have been in Otterburn. Whilst no witnesses were called at the inquest to say that they *had* seen the man, there were four witnesses who said that they had *not* seen him.

The evidence of Gladys Tatham and John Scott that he did not go into the Percy Arms cannot be construed as an indication that he was non-existent. If he was developing an obsession to ravish Evelyn Foster, he was hardly likely to have gone into the bar in search of someone else to give him a lift. Theoretically, he had a choice between an expensive ride to Ponteland and a free lift—but, in practical terms, money was not involved, since he had no intention of paying the hire-car fare.

The evidence of George Maughan, the Co-op assistant, and of John Thompson, the young farm labourer, has already been mentioned (see page 89), but parts of it are worth recapitulating.

Maughan said that he saw a car, which he took to be Evelyn Foster's Hudson, come along the road from Elishaw and pull up outside Foster's Garage; he 'saw no one in the car but the lady driving'. If a passenger had alighted from the car and walked towards the Percy Arms, then Maughan, walking with his wife in the opposite direction, should have seen him—but he remembered meeting only two persons between his house and the garage: William Blackham, the school-master, whom he recognised at the time, and John Thompson, whom he identified afterwards.

Whereas Maughan and his wife were walking out of the village, passing the garage on their right (they were going to the school where Maughan had a part-time job as caretaker), Thompson was coming into Otterburn from his place of work at Garretshiels, a farm lying between the Otterburn–Jedburgh road and Dere Street. Thompson's evidence was that he saw a car standing outside Foster's Garage as he passed: 'I took it to be Evelyn's, and heard a voice which I thought was hers. I did not see who she was talking to, only that he was wearing a pair of leggings. I believe that another man I saw near the car was Mr Maughan.'

In their unthinking way, the police—and later the coroner and the two solicitors at the inquest—accepted the evidence of Maughan and Thompson as being mutually corroborative. In fact, of course, it was nothing of the sort: rather, the shop assistant's account was at odds with that of the farm labourer, and vice versa.

Thompson came on to the Otterburn–Jedburgh road about a mile from the village, having cut across the fields from Garretshiels. If he had been overtaken by the car and had seen it pull up outside the garage, he would have said so. But what he said was: 'I passed Foster's Garage and saw a car standing there.' Clearly, then, the car must have been parked for some time before he came in sight of it. And just as clearly, Maughan, who saw the car drive up, could not possibly have met Thompson before reaching the garage.

Two questions arise: First, who was the man Maughan mistook for Thompson? And second, was the other man Maughan claimed to have seen really the schoolmaster? The reason for this second question is that, after the inquest, William Blackham confirmed that Maughan had seen him that night—but with the vital geographical proviso that the brief, passing-in-the-road encounter took place, not in the village, but between the garage and the school.

These points—coupled with Maughan's assertion that he passed the garage at about 6.30, half an hour before Evelyn Foster actually returned—throw such doubt on the shop assistant's evidence as to make it worthless. And the fact that Thompson was nowhere near the garage when the car pulled up, but arrived there after a passenger could have left the car and walked to—or towards—the Percy Arms, makes his evidence irrelevant. Indeed, the car he saw may not have been the Hudson ('I *took it to be* Evelyn's'); the female voice he heard may well have been that of Evelyn's sister Dorothy, who was serving petrol at the garage that night; and the 'man' he saw wearing 'a pair of leggings' may not have been a man at all, but Dorothy, who was wearing a soft felt hat that in the darkness could have been mistaken for a man's trilby, and thick stockings that might have looked like leggings.[6]

All the talk about the invisibility of the murderer stemmed from the invisibility of any witness at the inquest who had seen a strange man, or a man acting strangely, in Otterburn between the time of Evelyn Foster's return from Rochester and the time of her departure for Ponteland. Reasonably enough, the absence of such witnesses at the inquest was taken to mean that there *were* no witnesses to the presence of a stranger in the village. The inference was reasonable; the conclusion, however, was wrong.

Reference has already been made to Robert Townes, who gave important information to the police but was not called at the inquest. Just as one swallow does not make a summer, so the omission of one relevant witness is not necessarily a sign of disingenuous selectivity on the part of the police: there remains the comparatively charitable possibility of inefficiency. However, Townes was not the only person who should have been a witness but was not. There were at least three others.

Each of the three claimed to have seen a strange man in Otterburn at about seven o'clock on the night of the crime.

Luckily for justice—and perhaps uniquely in the annals of legal proceedings—the evidence of one of these missing witnesses was heard and dissected by eight members of the jury behind the closed door of the jury room. The evidence was given by the ninth member of the jury—who happened to be the missing witness.

George Sinclair, George Maughan's boss at the Co-op, made his statement to the police prior to receiving notice that he would be required to serve on the jury. Presumably, before he was sworn in (at the formal opening of the inquest on Thursday, 8 January), he did not point out to the coroner that if he were a juryman, he would be in the distinctly odd position of having to consider his own evidence as well as that of other witnesses in reaching a verdict. Sinclair is a common name in Northumberland, and this may explain why the police apparently never realised that the statement-maker and the juryman were one and the same person; if they *had* made the connection, they would surely have asked for Sinclair to be released from the jury and, with no choice in the matter, would have included him among the witnesses at the inquest.

Sinclair's statement was to the effect that as he left the Co-op at about seven o'clock, having stayed behind after closing time to check stocks, he caught sight of a stranger lurking in the shadows of the post-office, next door. (From the post office, Foster's Garage was in clear view.) The man moved hurriedly in the direction of the Percy Arms as Sinclair approached him.

By a curious coincidence, the two other missing witnesses were both schoolmistresses. One was Miss Annie Carruthers, who taught at the village of Elsdon.[7] Soon after seven o'clock, she was cycling through Otterburn. As she crossed the bridge, with the Percy Arms on her left, a man ran into the road, waving at her to stop. He asked if she could tell him the time of the next bus to Newcastle. Miss Carruthers said that she had no idea, and asked if he had enquired at the inn. 'The man then became offensive and made suggestive remarks, and I soon left him,' she said afterwards. Her recollection of the man's appearance tallied with Evelyn Foster's description of the murderer.

The other missing witness was Miss Mary Ferry, William Blackham's assistant at the village school. She called at the Percy Arms at about quarter-past seven to collect a pound of sausages that had been brought in on the bus from Hexham and deposited on the reception table by Tommy Rutherford. As she started to cross the bridge on her way home, something told her that she was being watched. Looking to her right, she saw a man standing beneath a tree on the embankment of the river. She stopped for a moment, supposing that the man would be someone she knew; then, realising that he was a stranger, went on her way at a discreetly faster pace. Whether she was afterwards able to describe the man is not known.

Almost anything is possible, of course. Each of these three witnesses —George Sinclair, Miss Carruthers, Miss Ferry—may have seen a different man rather than the same man at different times; perhaps the law of averages went berserk, and for ten minutes or so a village street, normally almost deserted on a winter evening, was inundated with strange men. Or maybe the three witnesses saw the same man—but a man who, by the sheerest of sheer chance, resembled a concocted description of a figmentary creature: a man who, at exactly the right time, behaved in a way the man described by Evelyn Foster might have done, had he existed outside the frontiers of her imagination.

Without invoking one of these slender possibilities—or rather, virtual *im*possibilities—the contention that the murderer was never seen, and therefore did not exist, cannot be sustained.

Twenty months after the burning of Evelyn Foster, at a place about a hundred miles from Wolf's Nick, there was another 'blazing car murder'. Very briefly, the facts of this case are as follows:

In 1929 Frederick Morton, the 24-year-old managing director of a cattle factoring company, employed a man named Ernest Brown as groom at the stables of his home near Huddersfield in Yorkshire. Though only 31, Brown was a widower. He was reasonably educated, personable and, away from the equestrian milieu, a natty dresser. Within a short time of his arrival—a matter of weeks, it seems—Morton's wife, Dorothy, who by all accounts was an attractive and athletic young woman, enlarged the definition of the term 'mistress of the house' to include sexual relations with him; she subsequently admitted that she 'did not resist' his first advances.

After about a year of this Chatterleyesque affair, during which time the determinedly unfaithful Mrs Morton also consorted with an embarrassment of rich local adulterers, she made it plain to the groom, either by words or lack of deeds, that she wanted to end the relationship. Brown did not take kindly to this rebuff; according to Mrs Morton, 'he became threatening, and I was very frightened'. Faced with a choice between submitting to Brown's sexual demands and telling her husband the whole sordid story, she decided on the former course, limiting the groom's visits to her bedroom by finding excuses for being away from the house more often when Frederick Morton was not there. From the start of the affair, Brown had exhibited the excessive jealousy of the person who has no legal or moral right to be jealous; now frustration, and the rage which it induced, combined with the jealousy, making him at times appear mentally deranged. Of the people associated with the house, only Morton—his mind engrossed in the business of selling cattle and the pleasure of hunting foxes—remained unaware of, or perhaps unconcerned with, the oddities of Brown's behaviour. The groom did his work well enough; this, to Morton, was all that mattered.

Just one or two events in the next couple of years need to be mentioned. In 1931 Dorothy Morton gave birth to a child, and a young woman called Ann Houseman was employed as nurse-companion. Early in 1933 the Mortons moved to Saxton Grange, an isolated farm outside Towton, a village to the south of Tadcaster in Yorkshire. Ann Houseman and Ernest Brown went with them, the groom's quarters being a wooden hut near the farmhouse.

In June 1933, Brown threw up his job in a fit of pique at being asked to mow a lawn, a task which to him seemed intentionally demeaning on Morton's part. Dorothy Morton must have been delighted at the prospect of no further sexual chores other than those imposed by her husband. The delight, however, was short-lived. After three or four days, Brown returned to Saxton Grange and implicitly threatened to kill her if she did not get her husband to reinstate him. 'He had his hand to his throat,' Mrs Morton stated at the trial, 'and this suggested to me that he was going to strangle me if I did not get him back.' She telephoned Morton who, after some argument, agreed to re-employ Brown—not as groom but as an odd-job man. Morton may have thought there was poetic justice in offering Brown a job that encompassed more lowly tasks than lawn-mowing. Certainly, Brown believed that the offer was motivated by spite. Even so, he accepted. A vindictive hatred was now added to the feelings of jealousy and frustration. Brown informed other workers at the farm that he intended to 'clout the little bugger one of these nights,' and on another occasion shouted: 'I can wreck this place, and I shall do it.' The hatred of Morton was apparent to everyone at the farm apart from Morton himself, in whose presence Brown assumed a mask of servitude.

On 5 September Morton drove to Oldham in a Chrysler saloon, one of the two cars he kept at Saxton Grange (the other was an Essex, almost identical to the Hudson Super-Six). He was away for most of the day. So was Brown, who was out driving a horse-box.

Brown met Dorothy Morton in the yard when he returned at about half-past eight. He asked her where her husband was, and she replied that he was not yet back from Oldham. He then asked how she had spent the day. On hearing that she had gone swimming in the river at Wetherby with a man whom he considered a rival for her affections, Brown attacked her, knocking her to the ground.

'I tried to shout for help,' Mrs Morton said at the trial. 'He tried to push me into the horse-box. Eventually Ann came—but just before, Brown pushed me into the barn. He was there trying to strangle me. His thumbs were on my throat, and he was pushing my head right back. I heard Ann approaching, and Brown pushed me away, at the same time putting his fingers to his mouth. I understood he did not want me to speak to Ann. Ann asked me if I had called out, and I said "No". Ann and I went into the house.'

Shortly afterwards, the two women heard a shotgun being discharged close to the kitchen window; Brown came into the kitchen a few minutes later and volunteered the information that he had been shooting rats. At quarter to ten the nurse-companion answered a telephone call from someone in Carlisle who wanted to speak to Morton. She suggested that the caller should ring again in fifteen minutes. This he did, but by then the line was dead; post office engineers afterwards established that the line was cut some time before ten o'clock.

The women went to their bedrooms, but neither of them undressed. At half-past eleven they heard the sound of a car's engine. Hoping that Morton had returned, they ran down to the hall. When the front door eventually opened, however, it was Brown who entered the house. 'The boss has been in and gone out again,' he said. Doing their best to hide their fear, Dorothy Morton and the nurse engaged Brown in casual conversation until midnight, when he left the house again.

The women went back upstairs, Mrs Morton locking herself in the bathroom, Ann Houseman keeping a look-out for Brown from her bedroom window. When the nurse saw Brown crossing the yard to the back door, she ran to join Mrs Morton. They stayed in the bath-room for an hour, listening to the sounds of the man moving about downstairs. The sounds ceased, and the women slipped across the landing to Ann Houseman's room.

At half-past three they heard small explosions and crackling sounds from outside the house. Parting the curtains, Mrs Morton saw that the garage on the far side of the yard was ablaze. They rushed to the tele-phone, found that the line was dead, and ran upstairs again. Mrs Morton picked up her child, and they ran out of the house and into the fields, where they hid beneath a hedge. By now, the garage was an inferno; the night sky was reddened by the flames. From the hedge, the women saw Brown rushing around in the yard, releasing horses from the outbuildings adjoining the garage. Later, they struggled across the fields to the village of Towton, about half a mile away, to give the alarm; while on their way, they were passed by Brown driving the horse-box along the road.

The ex-groom returned to the farm and looked on as the firemen fought the blaze. 'By God,' he said, staring at the garage, 'if the boss is in there, he'll never be seen again.'

Not until 9 am was it possible to get close enough to the garage to examine the debris. The remains of two cars were dragged into the yard. In the front passenger seat of the Chrysler saloon was a mass of charred flesh and bone, part of a man's body; the head, arms and lower limbs had been cremated, but bunches of keys and a unique platinum-and-diamond ring were sufficient to identify the dead man as Frederick Morton.

In a statement to the police, Brown said that his employer had returned home drunk at half-past eleven ('He was the clever side out' was the expression used by Brown to describe Morton's drunkenness). Morton had put the car away, but had told Brown that he intended to go out again. Brown claimed that he had said good-night to Morton, who was still sitting in the car, and had then gone to bed. He added that Morton was a heavy smoker and that he had sometimes slept in the car in the garage.

Brown was arrested immediately after the results of the post-mortem examination were imparted to the police. The examination established that Morton was dead before his body was burned. In the one small part of the chest that had escaped the flames, the pathologist found shotgun pellets and a scrap of gun-wad, the latter indicating a shot at close range. At Brown's trial, which was before Mr Justice Humphreys at Leeds Assizes on 11–13 December 1933, Crown counsel declared: 'If ever fate played a murderer a dirty trick, it did so here. Had the wound been in the upper part, it would never have been discovered.'

The jury accepted the Crown case, which was that Morton had returned to Saxton Grange, not at 11.30, as Brown claimed, but about two hours before; that Brown, immediately after shooting Morton, had fired a second shot nearer the house so that the rat-shooting explanation could be used in case anyone had heard the first shot; and that when he believed that the two women in the house were asleep, he had poured petrol over the body and around the garage and set fire to it. In sentencing Brown to death, Mr Justice Humphreys described him as 'a cruel and brutal murderer'.

I have tried to give only the bare details of the Saxton Grange case. The reader, however, may wonder why I have bothered to give any details at all. The reason is that there are certain common denominators, all but one of them admittedly slender, between Ernest Brown and the murderer of Evelyn Foster.

Apart from the obvious connection of two 'blazing car murders', Evelyn Foster's description of her passenger's accent as 'like Tyneside—not broad Tyneside but north country' could have applied to Brown's accent, for he was born at Huddersfield and spent part of his childhood at Byker, an inner suburb of Newcastle. Evelyn Foster's murderer was 'a bit of a knut'—in other words, sartorially elegant: so was Brown—who, according to press reports of his trial, was just about the best dressed man in court (a pity that it is not possible to whisper in print: the fact that a bowler hat was part of the 'uniform' of a groom deserves such under-emphasis). Both Evelyn Foster's murderer and Ernest Brown knew how to drive a car; though nowadays this would be unremarkable, in 1931 only a minority of men possessed such knowledge.

On Morton's behalf, Brown attended horse and cattle sales around the country, particularly in the far-northern English counties and across the border into Scotland. I have been unable to discover whether Brown was away at a sale on 6 January 1931. *If* he was—and if the sale took place anywhere near Jedburgh—then his best route back to Huddersfield would have been via Newcastle, the claimed destination of Evelyn Foster's murderer.

Taken together, these similarities and possibilities fall far short of providing even a tenuous basis for the assumption that Ernest Brown was a double-murderer. But the reader may feel that they derive a sort of reflected strength from Brown's final utterance before he was hanged at Armley Gaol, Leeds, on 6 February 1934.[8] He was on the scaffold, pinioned and masked, when the chaplain put forward the suggestion that his soul would profit from a brief—and, more to the point, prompt—confession of criminous sins. It seems reasonable to presume that most men in Brown's situation would not have felt much like talking. He, however, spoke back to the chaplain, saying either three words—'Ought to burn'—or one: 'Otterburn'. The executioner allowed him no time to elaborate.

Doesn't 'ought to burn' seem the least likely alternative? The remark is in the wrong tense for it to have been a vindictive reference to Frederick Morton; and it is hard to believe that Brown, having shown no remorse during his time in the condemned cell, would have contended that the mode of his execution should have been in apposition to a crime which he had steadfastly protested he did not commit. Of course, if Brown's response to the chaplain's well-meaning suggestion was the single word 'Otterburn', this does not necessarily mean that he was confessing to the murder of Evelyn Foster—or, if he was, that he was telling the truth and not indulging in an inverted form of braggadocio. Except in the ultimate sense, the scaffold was not notable for having a reformative effect on its temporary occupants; on the other hand, the gossip of capital punishment contains several stories of condemned men who treated the scaffold as a stage, as a place for a final performance before an invited audience, and who built up their parts by claiming credit for crimes they could not have committed.

All one can say is that Ernest Brown *may* have been Evelyn Foster's murderer. He was certainly capable of the crime;[9] in some respects, he resembled the description of the criminal; he appears to have been thinking of Otterburn at a time when his mind should have been concentrating wonderfully on something quite different.

What I am about to say will, I know, offend some readers as being reactionary and savage; I make no apology. I wish that there was evidence—incontrovertible evidence—that Ernest Brown was responsible for what happened at Wolf's Nick: not only for the intellectual pleasure of a tidy solution but also for the emotional delight in knowing that a man who escaped the consequences of one heinous crime was hanged for another two years later. In the absence of such evidence, I just hope that if Evelyn Foster's murderer is still alive, he has experienced tragedies considerable enough, and with sufficient frequency, to make him often wish that he were dead; I hope that if he is already dead, he has found out about hell-fire.

There is no way of knowing why certain things stay bright in the mind while others, perhaps more important or seemingly memorable, become so smudged that one cannot be sure whether one is remembering the reality or only a previous memory of it.

Two things I remember, and shall remember, with especial clarity from my re-examination of the Foster case.

One of the memories is of something said by Margaret Foster during my first meeting with Evelyn's sisters in the living-room of The Kennels. They have never before spoken about the case to an outsider, and for a time the conversation is constrained, embarrassed by silences. It is after a silence, yet in a voice so quiet that the silence seems unbroken, that Margaret says:

'We have thought about what happened ever since, but never for a moment have we doubted that Evie was murdered. Her death was made more terrible by other people's doubts. We were just young then, but that night made us old.'

The other memory is of Evelyn Foster's grave, which I see as if it were a picture-postcard in my mind. The black marble headstone, polished by the winds of many winters, looks as new as those on the surrounding graves of members of the family who have died more recently: Mrs Foster in 1951, Joseph a year later, Gordon in 1968.

Each Christmas, a holly wreath is placed on the grave. Though it might serve two purposes of remembrance, the wreath, because of custom, is removed on Twelfth Night, leaving the grave bare for the anniversary of Evelyn Foster's death.

1  In *A Reasonable Doubt*, Cresset Press, 1960.

2  Known cases of self-immolation are so rare, both in Great Britain and the United States of America, that they are not given a separate entry in national statistics of suicide.

3  *Pathological Firesetting*, Lewis, N. D. C., and Yarnell, H., Coolidge Foundation (New York), 1951.

4  Until Rouse's appeal was dismissed on 23 February 1931, the *sub-judice* rule constrained journalists from adumbrating a connection between the two cases; surprisingly, however, the possible connection is not referred to in any article that I have seen that was published after that date.

An article in the *Newcastle Evening Chronicle* of 19 February 1931 suggests that Evelyn Foster's murderer copied his *modus operandi* from an episode in *The W Plan*, a best-selling novel of espionage by Graham Seton (Thornton Butterworth, 1929), in which a British spy murders a German soldier, puts the victim in a car, runs the car over an embankment, and then sets fire to it. Helen Normanton, in her Introduction to *Trial of Alfred Arthur Rouse* (Hodge, Edinburgh, 1931), makes the same suggestion apropos of Rouse.

5  On 17 January 1931, the *Newcastle Evening Chronicle* carried the following report under the sub-heading, ONE CAR UNTRACED:

> The police, it is stated, have now accounted for every car known to have passed through Jedburgh on the day of the crime, except one, and that one, it is thought, was the one in which Miss Foster's assailant came to Otterburn.
>
> The occupants, it is believed, were two men and a woman who stayed at a hotel in Jedburgh for lunch, and left the town about 4 o'clock in the afternoon on their way South.
>
> The police attach much importance to this, as one of the two men has been described as a small man of dark complexion, and wearing dark clothes, which, it will be remembered, is the type of man Miss Foster described on her death-bed.

So far as I have been able to check, the police did not deny this story, and I have come across no subsequent report of the occupants of the car being traced.

6  According to villagers who are old enough to remember the case, the evidence given by both Maughan and Thompson differed in vital respects from the accounts they gave in conversation on the day after the crime.

At the inquest, Mrs Foster was so taken aback by Maughan's revised version that she involuntarily rose to her feet, saying, 'Oh, no!' Mr Bates ordered her to sit down, and refused to listen when she tried to explain to him the reason for her interruption. The reason was this: On the morning of 7 January, Maughan apparently told George Sinclair and customers at the Co-op that on the previous night, while walking from his home to the school, he had passed *three* men: William Blackham; a man whom he did not know who was standing inside the lich-gate of the church; and John Thompson, whom he had met *a quarter of a mile outside the village.*

It is said that, also on 7 January, Thompson told fellow farm-workers at Garretshiels that, the night before, he had seen Evelyn Foster's Hudson *passing the school* on the way to Otterburn just as he was coming on to the road.

7 She later married John Robson, the bus driver who gave evidence at the inquest of seeing Evelyn Foster's Hudson at Raylees.

8 The execution, originally fixed for 1 February, was postponed on 30 January in view of information placed before the Home Secretary by Brown's solicitor, pointing to some history of insanity in the prisoner's family. The Home Secretary directed a medical inquiry to be held into Brown's mental condition, under section 2(4) of the Criminal Lunatics Act 1884. The inquiry was made by Dr (later Sir) Norwood East, Medical Commissioner of HM Prisons, and Dr H. P. Foulerton, Medical Superintendent of Broadmoor Criminal Lunatic Asylum.

9 Prior to being found guilty of the murder of Frederick Morton, Brown's criminal record comprised convictions for the comparatively minor crime of theft (twice) and for being drunk and disorderly (six times).

# APPENDIX

## BRIEF MECHANICAL SPECIFICATIONS OF THE HUDSON SUPER-SIX

DIMENSIONS  Overall length, 13ft 6in; overall width, 5ft 5in; overall height, 5ft 10in; road clearance, 9in.

MAXIMUM SPEEDS ON GEARS  1st, 24mph; 2nd, 34mph; top, 63mph.

FUEL CONSUMPTION  20–22mpg (approx.).

ENGINE  Six-cylinder Super-Six type, F-head, intake valves in head, exhaust valves in side; cylinders cast en bloc; separate cast aluminium crankcase; bore and stroke, $3\frac{1}{2} \times 5$in, silent chain front-end drive; tax rating 29·4 horsepower.

CRANKSHAFT  Special patented Super-Six design, fully compensated to prevent vibration; the Hudson engine may be operated with absolute safety and with perfect balance at speeds as high as 5,000 rpm. Four bronze-backed babbitt-lined main bearings. Light-weight aluminium alloy pistons, circulating splash lubrication; ventilated crankcase; oil capacity: 7 quarts.

FUEL SYSTEM  Vacuum feed from $15\frac{1}{2}$ gallon tank at rear. Marvel car-burettor, automatic air valve and manual heat control. Improved manifold design ensures starting and economy in fuel consumption; petrol gauge on instrument panel.

COOLING  Forced circulation by centrifugal pump; cellular radiator. Water temperature controlled by manually operated radiator shutters; capacity of system $5\frac{1}{2}$ gallons.

ELECTRICAL SYSTEM  2-unit 6-volt starting and lighting with 120 ampere hour battery. Ignition provided with automatic and manual advance controls.

CLUTCH  Single-disc type, with cork inserts running in oil and sealed in oil-tight housing. Annular ball-type thrust bearing, clutch unit completely balanced.

TRANSMISSION  Selective sliding gear type; three speeds forward, one reverse, ball and roller bearings, alloy steel gears, heat-treated; transmission lock; tubular propeller shaft with spicer universal joints; fully balanced.

FRONT AXLE  Heavy 1-beam type.

REAR AXLE  Semi-floating mounted in roller bearings, spiral bevel gears; extra-large pinion bearings, Hotchkiss drive (through rear springs).

BRAKES  Bendix 4-wheel mechanical brakes, expanding-shoe type, self-energising, adjustable and equalised for wear. Hand brake: rear internal expanding.

SPRINGS  Special alloy steel, semi-elliptic, front and rear. Front 39in long. Rear 57½in long. Adjustable shackles.

FRAME  Heavy channel side members 7in deep with 6 rigid cross members.

STEERING  Roller-disc-type gear, fully adjustable; special thrust bearings in heads of front wheel spindles.

WHEELS AND TYRES  Wood-artillery-type wheels with steel-felloe mounting. 31 × 6in low-pressure, balloon-type, non-skid tyres.

WHEELBASE  127⅜in.

EQUIPMENT INCLUDES:

| | | |
|---|---|---|
| Parking lights | Scuttle ventilator | Radiator shutters |
| Rear-view mirror | Transmission lock | Automatic windshield |
| Motometer | Sun visor | cleaner |
| Dome light | Tyre carrier | Speedometer |
| Stop light | Petrol gauge on instrument panel | |

# INDEX